earth is your sweet spot

A Woman's Guide to Living Beautifully

ellae elinwood and mary lanier

Confluence Books

Ashland, Oregon

Cover photo by Marina Filipovic Marinshe
Cover and interior design by Confluence Book Services

First Edition 2012

Library of Congress Cataloging-in-Publication Data

Elinwood, Ellae.

 Earth is your sweet spot : living beautifully, a woman's guide /
by Ellae Elinwood and Mary Lanier.

     p. cm.

 ISBN 978-1-935952-03-9 (pbk.)

1. Beauty, Personal. 2. Women--Health and hygiene. I. Lanier,
Mary. II. Title.

 RA778.E395 2011

 613'.04244--dc23

                                    2011025701

TABLE OF CONTENTS

DEDICATION

This book came to fruition thanks to the love, insight, and support of our friends, families, and loved ones. Thank you.

A tribute to Katie Garland Nobel for her hours of labor on the formulation of the book. We so appreciate you, Katie.

Thanks to . . .

- ↬ Gregge Tiffen: Teacher, Mentor, and friend. You first seeded this wisdom, then stepped back, and let it bloom.

- ↬ Vickie: Without your silent support, this book would never have lifted off the ground.

- ↬ Tom: You are always reminding me how much fun it is to be a woman.

- ↬ Bruce and Paul: Your commitment to evolving consciousness has made this book possible.

- ↬ Steve Scholl: Our publisher, for sharing our vision and then giving it life.

Our daughters and granddaughters: Katie, Juliette, Kirsten, Chelsea, Karin, Katherine Grace, and Elizabeth Brynn. A wonderful Earth infuses you with love, wisdom, support, and peace that asks only acceptance.

JOIN US ONLINE

Please join us online, and tell us how you love to connect with the Earth.

Earth Is Your Sweet Spot's official website:
www.earthisyoursweetspot.com

Twitter:
www.twitter.com/earthsweetspot

Facebook:
www.facebook.com/pages/Earth-is-Your-Sweet-Spot/362832226136

Ellae Elinwood:
www.ellaeblogs.blogspot.com

Mary Lanier:
www.marylanier.blogspot.com

Dear Readers,

Thank you for taking the time to read this book. We want to let you know that the information herein is not a teaching, it is a remembering . . . a remembering that we are all collectively doing together.

In Gratitude,

Ellae and Mary

CHAPTER ONE

VITALITY

- ❧ *Revolutionize yourself.*
- ❧ *Radiate balance.*
- ❧ *Discover an infinite capacity for renewal.*
- ❧ *Unmask lifelong tools for youthful looks, health, and vibrancy.*

The simple journey to inner abundance begins with Earth. Earth is female, and as a woman, you are one with her.

Transform and influence your life, become exquisite. Learn the tools to positively direct your life. Join with Earth's loveliness and unlock your own.

Is this a lot of work? No, you're already there. You have just been distracted in a state of temporary forgetfulness. Rediscover your source and allow Earth to become a friend, a guide, a fountain of nurturing, wisdom, and renewal.

Elegant Balance

Seek and always find your inspiration in Earth: birds, mountains, trees, flowers, viruses, and bacteria . . . an endless list. All of life, microscopic to enormous, burgeons unrestrained. Earth's nature is consistent, uncompromising, and breathtakingly beautiful. In the midst of this elegant balance, nature reproduces herself. With an uninterrupted brilliance, Earth adapts, renews, sustains, endures, and expands.

Your Source of Vitality

Earth is your source of vitality, the wellspring filling you up, facilitating your ability to connect with your surroundings.

One way you can realize your union with her is through your personal memories.

In your busy world, or your still world, Earth's magnificence envelops and merges with you.

Reflect.
When was your attention drawn to her?
What are your private memories?

Here are some of ours...
- Inhaling the first smells of morning.
- Lying in sweetly scented grasses.
- Hearing the hum of insect life.
- Feeling gritty sand between the toes.
- Watching a bird in mid-flight.
- Eyeing a floating butterfly.
- Smelling the fragrance of a pink rose.
- Stunned by a view.

Earth is alive. She interacts
with each one of us and in these
moments, we are participating
in a back and forth communication.
Start now: Here is a fullproof method . . .
Nature loves to be appreciated.

Ellae: *"I remember the very first time I felt Earth's inclusion. I was little, ten, and it was summer break, a hot Ohio summer. I had joined with Earth, eating newly planted soybeans with deep contentment—contentment which peaked unexpectedly. Lying out in a patch of shade I relaxed. A comfort that knew no loneliness or longing filled me. I was complete. I became the comfort and slept. A magical moment fused into my cellular memory. I had 'grounded' and started my journey into womanhood."*

What is "being grounded" and what does it entail? And, more importantly, how much time will it take? Being grounded deepens and stabilizes the gifts that Earth continually has to offer. A first step might be to acknowledge and become tuned in to the scientifically measurable resonance of the Earth.

"I have touched a place where the Earth is breathing."
RUMI

EARTH'S RESONANCE:
A BRIEF HISTORY

Earth has her own energetic resonance that is a discernible pulse. These energies form a heartbeat, radiating from her and graciously including us in this energetic environment. Earth's resonance has been documented by physicists and other scientists, while indigenous cultures have held drumming ceremonies as a way to merge with and revere this resonance. In the 1950's, the German physicist Professor W. O. Schumann, from the Technical University of Munich, discovered electromagnetic waves in the Earth's atmosphere. Dr. Schumann and his student Herbert König proved that these measurable resonances maintain a frequency of about 7.83 Hz. These resonances, now known as the Schumann Resonances (SR), are electromagnetic pulses. They are generated by electrical discharges such as lightning.[1]

SCHUMANN RESONANCES AND HUMAN HEALTH

Many scientists, physicists, and other curious minds have studied the Schumann Resonances and found a fascinating correlation between the Schumann Resonances and their effects on human health.

A physician named Dr. Ankermueller recognized the relationship between the SR and human brainwaves. Doctoral candidate Herbert König researched this connection and discovered that the main frequency produced by Schumann Resonances is almost exactly attuned to the frequency of alpha rhythm brainwaves.[2]

---

1. See Ingrid Pastl-Dickenson's overview of the Schumann Resonance online at www.earthbreathing.co.uk/sr.htm
2. N. J. Cherry, "Human intelligence: The brain, an electromagnetic system synchronised by the Schumann Resonance signal," *Medical Hypotheses* 60 (June 2003): 843-44.

He believed that the human brain and the Earth's resonance are therefore intimately connected. Some studies have proven that human health is dependent on these resonances: Professor R. Wever, of the Max Planck Institute for Behavioural Physiology, researched this by creating a vacuum in an underground bunker, free of any magnetic fields. Young volunteers lived in this bunker for several weeks and experienced headaches, emotional stress, and other illnesses. Their "circadian rhythms," i.e. their daily cycles of biological activity based on a 24-hour period, were severely disturbed. Early astronauts experienced similar symptoms, and space shuttles now simulate Schumann Resonances.

THE IMPORTANCE OF THE SCHUMANN RESONANCES

These experiments bring to light the tremendous value of Earth's resonance. Human beings and mammalian brains need to stay in consistent connection with the Schumann Resonances in order to experience optimal health and emotional balance. However, as electromagnetic devices have become more popular in modern civilization, the Schumann Resonances are weakening. The static of our electronic devices are competing with the strong resonance emanating from Earth.

Dr. Wolfgang Ludwig proved this when he attempted to measure the SR. Dr. Ludwig actually discovered that he could not obtain accurate measurements near cities due to the electromagnetic signals of electronic devices like cell phones, computers, etc. Ludwig went underground into mines and above ground on the ocean to access strong Schumann Resonances.[3]

We believe that human beings, and especially women, can consciously engage Earth's resonance in order to experience optimal wellness, emotional, physical, and biochemical balance.

---

3. See Ingrid Pastl-Dickenson, www.earthbreathing.co.uk.

Remember Earth and Earth's Resonance

Human beings are always connected to Earth's resonance. We are one with her. We simply need to tune out the static and the distractions and wake up to Earth: She is ever present and supportive.

Earth is alive, very alive. Look around you: Nature, in all of her vastness and perfection, is everywhere.

Like Earth, women have the gift of reproduction and as a result our bodies are especially easily attuned to Earth's resonance. A woman can remember the ease of her connection to Earth at any time by placing her receptive body close to Earth and her creatures. Even if you do not live in a place where it is safe to to go outside, you can join with Earth from the comfort of your home.

Next, you can offer appreciation to Earth and her beauty. Admire the cloud formations. Give thanks to the piercing pink hues in a chrysanthemum flower.

A plant emerging through the pavement. A bird riding the winds.

If your home is your safe place, cozy up to a beloved house pet or offer a gift of thanks by nurturing a plant.

It is important to express admiration and appreciation to Earth and to receive, and even perceive, her resonance. Engaging with Earth is never a sucking, pulling, or drawing up experience. Part of our distractedness is that we have forgotten how to engage and appreciate Earth.

Simply open yourself to her. Engaging with Earth is natural as you open your awareness and remember what has always been there. Open to her from a state of shared beauty and gratitude.

Women can also learn the art of engaging and appreciating Earth from certain men.

A woman loves it when a man knows how to engage her, make her laugh, appreciate her, and bring out the wonderful and unexpected qualities within her. The man does all of these things without ever depleting the woman. Instead, he enhances and appreciates her unique loveliness. And when a woman appreciates the man for this form of engagement, he is filled with joy. They are simultaneously delighted and both of their days have just improved. A woman can make a man's day by appreciating him.

This is the way that we as women can engage with Earth and benefit from her vitality by understanding her. We can gain her attention through appreciating her. We can communicate with her and celebrate her loveliness. Just like us, Earth doesn't like to be depleted, she wants to be valued for her willing generosity. Then thanked with an acknowledgement.

A REMEMBERING

Your connection to Earth and her resonance isn't something you have to learn, you already know it: It's as if it is already embedded in your feminine cellular makeup.

Your conscious "discovery" of Earth and her resonance is simply a remembering.... a remembering that we are all collectively doing together.

Earth is everybody's sweet spot.

APPRECIATE AND COMMUNICATE WITH EARTH

Much as we nurture relationships with the people we love, we can nurture our relationship with Earth. Earth is alive and the more we talk to and communicate with her, the more vibrant she becomes.

> ✦ *Try: Looking up at the sky. What do you see?*
> *Gorgeous, fluffy clouds? Mist? Birds?*
> *Pick an element of nature, and let Earth know*
> *how lovely she is.*

Ellae: *"I created a small ritual that I will briefly describe below. Feel free to try it, to make it your own."*

NURTURE EARTH RITUAL

We each have a unique capacity to nurture a personal and personally rewarding relationship to Earth. This relationship is a special opportunity to remember your connection to Earth and her resonance. It is mutually supportive and healing. Earth is already wounded. You can tend to her at any time, and you will both benefit.

With this in mind, I have been comforting the Earth. I have been encouraging and tender with her flowers, her trees and grasses as I care for them. As I see, touch, and smell each one I am giving comfort and encouragement; I run my hands over the dirt and grasses as if they are her skin, which they are. I offer understanding, sympathy, and support. This is exactly the care I would give one of you if you were not well.

Learn to be very aware of your contact with the Earth under your feet, as you lean against a tree, or share amazement at the beauty of a spray of water, the pure color of a flower, wind swaying a tree. Know that you are simultaneously contributing to Earth's loveliness and your own.

I find comfort that despite her stresses Earth's capacity for renewal is enormous. Earth still is able to maintain areas of such beauty and balance.

The snow still glistens on the mountain top, the spring flowers are still fabulous, forests are majestic, babies in all shapes and sizes are popping out. We are surrounded by her beauty and generosity.

EARTH IS OPEN

Earth is open to all. She is non-denominational, non-sectarian, and accepting of all faiths, colors, and kinds. You can celebrate and appreciate your connection to her no matter your personal belief system. And, most importantly, you can make your relationship to her your own. You can craft your own personal beliefs into your unique connection to Earth. Her generosity knows no limits, so you can celebrate her any way you like!

LET EARTH BALANCE YOU

Open your body to receive her resonance. Let her ageless vitality refresh and balance you. You may feel the actual pulsation or you may not. If you don't feel it, it is still there doing the work of balancing and cleaning your energetic field.

START NOW

Explore connecting into Earth's resonance. Utilize the elements of Earth that are immediately around you.

You might begin with an animal or a houseplant.
Our editor described her interaction with her dog:

"I spent a few minutes this morning marveling over the softness of my miniature dachshund's ears and listening to her breathe. It made us both very happy."

MARGIE LAWSON

Interaction with animals, plants, and the natural world are the bridges that lead us to Earth's resonance.

TRANSFORM

A transformation occurs as you join with Earth's resonance, appreciate and communicate with her. You move from exhaustion to vitality, from internal dissonance to greater harmony. No longer as distracted, you are now closer to your own unique loveliness.

Imagine how this world would be if every woman walked and talked in her own unique femininity. We would pass from one inspirational woman to another. To be uniquely whole and lovely is the birthright of every woman. When grounded into Earth, a woman is in her true nature.

THE NATURE DEFICIT DISORDER TEST

How often do you take time to appreciate Earth? Try this test.

On a scale of 1 to 5, 5 being often, 1 being never:
Finish your day renewed…

How often do you finish your day renewed
  by life and sweetly tired?   _____

Exercise in a safe place outside?   _____

Take a deep and satisfying breath?   _____

Notice a bird's nest?   _____

Observe the trees in your area?   _____

Appreciate a local flower bed?   _____

Watch the change of a season?   _____
  For example summer to fall.

Nurture your plants and animals?   _____

Sit outside, relax, and open up?   _____

Let your animals nurture you back?   _____

SCORING:

50–40: You're there! You have nature integrated into your life.
This book will help you take the next step.
40–30: You're doing okay. But there is more pleasure awaiting you.
30–0: Smell the roses. Time to change.

Spend a little more time outside each day. Even if this is just
consistently slowing down the walk from the house to the
car. Admire. Interact. Enjoy. This is a simple pleasure with
great rewards.

Life is short but it is very wide.
ROBERT ALTMAN

VITALITY

EMOTIONAL EXCESS

In modern culture, many people no longer turn to Earth for revitalization and renewal. Perhaps you also no longer rely on her, and your Nature Deficit Disorder Test results reflect this. If you've lost your connection to her, you may feel fatigued, a lack of self-confidence, over-extended, or depleted. You have slid out of balance.

You may be in a personal state of emotional excess. This means that one emotion has overpowered the rest of your rich emotional life, and now dominates. Depending on your personal tendency, this emotion may be: fear, anger, anxiety, jealousy, sadness, depression, grief, ambition, fatigue, impatience, or sentimentality. Fear and anger most commonly reign supreme.

No matter what your personal tendency, the result is the same: The emotion becomes pervasive and guards its right to monopolize your health. You will remain compromised until you recognize your deficit and seek balance.

Accepting a full range of emotion is critical. To personally evolve and contribute to the evolution of others, it is important to experience a full emotional life, and consistently regain balance. Earth is your gateway to this stability.

INTEND TO BECOME CONNECTED

Spend meaningful time with Earth and develop the ability to feel an immediate difference in your core vitality and emotional health.

Interact with Earth

Many of us tap into resources such as therapy, doctors, spas, etc. to renew and replenish. These perfectly appropriate personal enhancers too often become temporary solutions.

It is only through harmonizing with Earth's vital resonance and realigning with her life-giving energy that true revitalization occurs. While the other solutions provide a fleeting sense of ease, rejuvenating through contact and communication with Earth is timeless.

Rekindle

When you link your body with Earth's resonance, you enhance your femininity and a natural balance is renewed. There are many practical ways to connect; the important thing is to coordinate your pulse with Earth through physical contact. Establish the intention to connect your physical body to Earth each day. This can be done by going for a walk, running your fingers through soil or sand, petting a loving animal, or nurturing an unhappy plant.

Mary: "I learned about the Schumann Resonances and connecting to Earth due to a personal illness I suffered from. I was at my wit's end and I had explored every avenue that modern medicine could offer... still I couldn't get better. Ellae, a longtime friend, recommended I begin going on hikes and connecting my physical body to the Earth. At the time my immune system was greatly compromised and I couldn't imagine walking down the street to get the mail, let alone going on a drawn out 'nature hike.' Still, I felt I had limited options and I started going on hikes.

"Something truly magical started happening. I experienced significant healing in my physical body and my emotional state of being changed. I went from being constantly bombarded by my thoughts and experiencing anxiety to dwelling in the lower half of my body, breathing, and knowing true peace. Eight years later, I am a different person. My enzymes have returned to healthy levels, and I gratefully have a clean bill of health.

"My connection to Earth and Earth's resonance is the primary relationship I nurture. This relationship fills me up, and has provided me with a truly abundant inner life that now manifests itself in my 'real life.' Does this mean my life is perfect and free of pain? No. Perhaps the opposite is true. In recent years I have experienced some of the most devastating heartaches. But I believe my connection to Earth has carried me through the pain. It continues to give me more room inside to breathe and brings me back to the beauty of life."

THE DAILY CONNECTION

It is the daily joining with Earth that's key. If you have five minutes . . . Give a plant a bit of admiration and a gentle touch. Enhance your garden.

↬ If you have twenty minutes . . . Go for a pleasurable walk outdoors. With each step, feel your feet touch the ground. Imagine the vibrations of each footstep resonating down into the deep root system beneath you.

↬ Inhale.

↬ Exhale.

↬ If you have an hour . . . Discover a quiet trail by your home.

Walk on the sand by the ocean. Amble through a wheat field. If you live in a big city, make your own trail: Meander on the sidewalks. Watch for insects, hidden plants, towering trees. Pay attention to the terrain. Marvel at nature's ability to display her right to exist anywhere and everywhere.

↬ If you live in an unsafe place, find a photo of your favorite element in nature—a mountain, a rose, or the beach. Let your five senses take you there. Imagine! Feel it, touch it, taste it. No matter where you are, appreciate the raw majesty of Earth.

↬ Start where you are. Start now.

As you set the intention to spend valuable time to connect into Earth each day, you may discover yourself making more time for interaction. Five minutes willingly becomes twenty. Twenty minutes becomes an hour.

↬ Stay open and receptive. Earth is calling you.

Connect In

↬ Find safe locations. A place that is quiet, even silent. Relax. Let your body open to this safety and soften.

↬ Feel the beat of your heart, and you may feel Earth's resonance. A slow, steady rhythm. As you open, you become more receptive.

↬ Enhance your receptivity. Lie on Earth for an hour, perhaps in your backyard, in a park, or on the sand by the ocean. Relax your mind.

↬ Sleep outside, if you are safe.

↬ Go for a walk.

Taking it Further

Imagine you are dragging a luxurious tail of your choice behind you. One day try an ostrich, another a peacock, alligator, monkey, kangaroo. Your choice. Have fun with it!

Let your energy trail below your waist. This visualization will help you drop your energy into the lower half of your body and bring an understanding of what it is to be grounded in Earth.

An Alchemist

Uncompromising and essential femininity creates a comfy body, a warm and confident emotional life, a clear mental purpose, and a profound spiritual maturity. A woman who aligns herself with Earth's pulse is an alchemist who takes the raw material of youth and weaves it into the gold of ongoing maturity. She lives the miracle of life.

16

References
For more information on the Schumann Resonances, consult these sources:

N. J. Cherry, 2002, "Schumann Resonances, a plausible biophysical mechanism for the human health effects of Solar/Geomagnetic Activity," *Natural Hazards* 26(3), pp. 279-331.

N. J. Cherry, 2003, "Human intelligence: The brain, an electromagnetic system synchronised by the Schumann Resonance signal," *Medical Hypotheses* 60(60):843-44.

J. A. Gray, 1982, *The Neuropsychology of Anxiety: An Enquiry into the Functions of the Septo-Hippocampal System.* Clarendon Press.

CHAPTER TWO

RECIPROCITY

THE LAW OF IMPERMANENCE

It is the nature of things—life, circumstances, and people—to be impermanent. Earth, too, is governed by the law of impermanence, but instead of yielding chaos, her impermanence creates an atmosphere of reciprocity and generates balance.

RECIPROCAL RELATING—EARTH'S WAY

Reciprocal energy is mutual giving and taking. Earth has no other way of relating. Everything that happens in nature is an act of reciprocity. Nothing is wasted.

Indigenous people have understood this and tried to maintain a lifestyle that continually restores reciprocity in their relationship to Earth. They regard Earth as a beautiful, living organism of great female power. The foundation of their way of life is to live in harmony with Earth's law of reciprocity. They do not see nature from the viewpoint of control and domination, but rather from the perspective of a life lived in balance with Earth's ways.

These communities make an effort to learn about her ways and live in harmony with her.

Everyone knows the destruction that nature can inflict and that she is indeed a force to reckon with.

Through their understanding of how to harmonize with her, they have generated resilient attitudes, and a safer environment for themselves throughout the ages.

EARTH'S WAY

All forms of life, including human life, are maintained in a constant balance with the whole of Earth's nature. When an animal dies, a trees falls, a baby is born, all of nature adjusts to this and rebalances. Her energies are in a state of constant flux.

Everything in nature is valuable. There is no waste. Nature responds with balance and reciprocal relationships thrive throughout her realm. This achieved state of balance then produces Earth's beautiful creativity, the cycle of life.

THE RESTORATION OF BALANCE

As a woman, you can mimic Earth's ways and respond to every life event with the intent to restore balance through reciprocity. You can manage your reactions and seek to respond from a point of balance.

FIGURE EIGHT

Imagine a figure eight on its side. Both sides are equal in size. This represents giving and receiving in reciprocity. It is this equality that produces balance.

This is true female power, creating and restoring mutuality so life can flourish.

The Emerging Balance

When responding reciprocally, you don't give more or less than the situation calls for. In the emerging balance, you can envision the figure eight and determine where your personal situation fits in.

You are free to upgrade your quality when you are in harmony with this law of nature.

Mimic Earth

Let Earth be your primary supportive relationship. Study her. Understand and integrate the reciprocity in action that you observe in nature.

Example: When a new mother breastfeeds, her breasts swell uncomfortably. Her baby then nurses from the breasts, receives vital nourishment, and the swelling goes down. This relieves the mother's pain and it also helps her lose weight and tightens her uterus. This is reciprocal relating in action.

Implementing Reciprocity

Ellae: "I have an Irish irritable side. Recently a friend got very aggressive and angry with me. She began yelling. Even though my personal tendency is to retaliate and fight back, I have learned over time that in these moments, it is important to stop and be quiet. So I listened to my friend and remained calm. Instead of matching aggression with aggression, I was still and receptive. The situation then easily resolved. Doing the balanced opposite enabled the restoration and rebalancing to begin.

"The opposite of this experience happened a few weeks ago. I was in a restaurant with my friend, Ted. The guy behind Ted banged his chair, Ted banged back. The guy banged Ted again, Ted banged back. This back and forth aggression escalated

until the waitress intervened and stopped a shouting match. Clearly this was mimicking but not reciprocal relating."

The Ultimate Challenge

The ultimate female task is to be deeply engaged in life without feeling consumed. Yet many women juggle a career, a family, a social and spiritual life, and end the day depleted: They do not feel luxuriously tired, satisfied with the activities and productivity of the day, grateful for a good night's rest, and exhilarated for what the next day will bring.

These women are sucked dry, exhausted, worn to shreds from the bouncing and racing around, the day's responsibilities, the kids screaming, the partner's demands.

Often in their depletion, they express non-creative ways of coping such as control, victimization, manipulation, competition, etc.

This is not Earth's way. When the laws of reciprocal relating are forgotten, a woman gives too much or too little. Lost and out of alignment with Earth, she loses her strength. She may choose to withdraw to recover, for example, by avoiding relationships, isolating herself from friends and loved ones. But this is an inadequate recovery tactic. She needs to return to her source and fill up.

Return to Your Source

↭ Reach down and scratch your dog's ears. Put your attention in your hands. Experience the mutual enjoyment.

↭ Nurture Earth.

↭ Look at a pine tree, nurture it with your eyes, even if you are looking through a window. Cherish the prickly, spiky branches, the oxygen it gives you.

⤷ Appreciate Earth.

⤷ Be grateful for a neighbor's beautiful organic garden without feeling envious.

FILL UP

⤷ Filling up is focusing your intent to engage, nurture, and appreciate.

Here are our favorite ways to return to our source and fill up:

Ellae: *"I like to nurture plants that are close to the house. I also have a family and pets, two cats, a dog, and a cockatoo. Our interactions connect me to Earth."*

Mary: *"For me, the ultimate experience of rebalancing occurs in the wildness of nature. Fortunately, I have chosen to live part time in San Francisco, where in thirty minutes I can leave my urban home and be on a mountain trail or by the ocean. Away from high-tension wires and buzzing motors, my body can relax and expand into the stillness and symmetry of the natural world. This allows me to return to my full life with renewed inner strength."*

YOUR OWN PERFECT WAY

List ideas to deepen your connection to Earth.

1. _____

2. _____

3. _____

4. _____

5. _____

Women have enormous influence on the level and type of consciousness that exudes from their homes, businesses, and relationships. When women act in reciprocity, life balances. There is no formula that promises to reveal how to learn and master the language of balance or reciprocity.

Trust yourself as you form your intent and make a commitment to be a conveyer of balance. Turn to Earth and observe nature. Draw your personal style from what you see.

You will improve over time. There is not one system. Each woman has her own perfect way.

Not in My House

Once a renowned African American author hosted a party at her house. A guest murmured a racial slur. She stopped and stood on her tiptoes. She pointed her finger at the guest and said, "Not in my house." This is a perfect example of reciprocal relating in action. Timing was of the essence here, and she didn't shrivel or falter. She stood up and spoke up.

Right Timing

Timing is everything, and a woman must trust herself in the moment, and appropriately respond to what comes her way.

Our Job

Our job is not to be all forgiving, all loving, and filled with endless compassion for the suffering created around us. Our job as women is to learn the laws of reciprocity and live by them.

Take a moment and reflect. Are your personal relationships balanced through reciprocity? Or are you currently struggling with an imbalanced relationship with a partner, child, grandchild, or friend? If imbalance exists, become aware of how you might restore balance and positively affect the current situation.

Sometimes in life, we sign up for something with an air of naiveté, not knowing what the opportunity calls for, or will call forth within us.

If we stick with the commitment and embrace the complexity, we choose to expand and become more competent.

Reciprocity in Action

A child is crying. You give a smile.

A tree has been cut down. You plant another.

A politician has squandered money.
You give to your favorite charity.

A friend has committed suicide.
You volunteer at a hospital and hold new babies.

An adolescent is lost in drug abuse. You give your love to a child who needs someone to believe in him or her.

A loved one has turned away from you. You take that love and portion it out to everyone you meet.

CHAPTER THREE

KRONOS & KAIROS

The Greeks had two types of time: *Kronos* and *Kairos*. Kronos is the constructed timing of humans. An example of Kronos would be: "I will meet you at five P.M." Kronos dominates in our culture. It possesses a sense of urgency. We are all very familiar with accepting Kronos time.

The other type of time is Kairos, the arrival of unbidden events. An example of Kairos would be: "I got a flat tire and am delayed." Kairos is the creation of a fresh opening. It brings an invitation to hone a new response.

Often we react with irritation to unplanned interruption. Kairos time is the timing of the Universe. Timing that teaches us through the unexpected: interactions, events, circumstances, journeys, delays, etc. These interruptions introduce the opportunity to respond in new ways. We are offered a moment in time to alter, upgrade, and incorporate new perceptions. We can let go of the aspects of life that have become useless and repetitive.

Repetition is the most negative state of existence, guaranteed to diminish vitality.

Some of the most common forms of repetition are: conditioned habits of response, procrastination, mental rigidity, addictions and emotionally driven behavior.

Repetition is: if you always do what you've always done, you'll always get what you've always gotten.

Kairos interruptions are often challenging. But these challenges provide us with opportunities to break up stale repetitions in our behavior, and learn new tools for life.

The goal is to encourage an ongoing sense of wonder—a wonder that could be yours if you walked down a path with the intention of seeing something new each time.

Mary: *"I remember riding in an old minibus on my way to an airport in Siberia. We hit a large pothole, and the front tire went flat. I sat there, agonizing over how I would be delayed, if I would miss my flight. I was caught up in Kronos time.*

A couple sitting next to me with their three-year-old daughter stood up and stepped off the bus. They sat down on the grass by the side of the road, and ate their picnic lunch. A few men sitting behind me began talking and laughing in Russian. Realizing I was powerless over the situation, and my angst wouldn't help me get to the airport any faster, I pulled out my book and snack. I relaxed into the moment, and turned the delay into a time I could enjoy."

CHANGE COMES LIKE A FLASH OF LIGHTNING

Unforeseen events, remarks by friends, even sudden emotional upsets can come out of nowhere and these experiences separate us from the familiar.

In Kairos time, it is important to step back and turn away from emotionally driven behavior. Take the necessary time to assess possible reactions. Choose the reaction that expresses the greatest amount of wisdom in interacting with the situation.

While repetitious responses create the same old-same old, wisdom facilitates a new response, an improvement. When the lightning strikes, it is an invitation to move into something new and let it teach you.

ALIGNMENT WITH EARTH'S ENERGIES

Spending valuable time in nature with the intent to align ourselves with the Earth's heartbeat and her resonance prepares us to open to the unexpected.

When coordinated with Earth's energies, it is easier to creatively meet these unexpected Kairos occurrences. Filling up through Earth enables us to have personally creative responses to the new challenges and opportunities.

- ✧ Mountains facilitate new perspectives.
- ✧ Lakes have a calming effect, encouraging acceptance.
- ✧ Rivers nudge you towards change.
- ✧ Flowers generate hopefulness.

Earth is there to guide you.

Ellae: "*The lightning flashed. My oldest daughter died unexpectedly at age thirty.*

"*She left behind her two wonderful small children. My choice was to return to my very lovely life or raise my grandchildren and participate in their struggle and healing. I walked the beach. Asked the ocean for guidance. Wept into the sand. Asked the mountains for strength. The answers came. I decided to embrace my grandchildren and go through our lives together. I left my complacent comforts and held with that which was, at first, difficult.*

"*It has become clear over time that my grandchildren drew me into a joyous life. Whereas my lovely contained life would have only drawn me into my deep sorrow. Earth comforted and inspired me as I made my choice. The choice was right for us all.*"

FINDING YOUR ALIGNMENT

Choose to balance variety and consistency.

If you go on daily walks and usually walk north, walk south.

If you generally go left, go right.

If your eyes always fall onto the same view, expand it.

If you're someone who usually looks at the hole, begin looking at the whole.

Expand. Grow.

Use Ellae's favorite Kairos slogan: "*Okay, fresh approach!*"

Let your connection with Earth help you embrace life's changes.

KRONOS & KAIROS

THE FIVE SENSES

One of the most wonderful ways to expand awareness and move into Kairos time is through the Five Senses. Humanity evolved the Five Senses to better understand the rhythms of Earth and facilitate survival. Nowadays survival isn't the big issue, but we can still use the Five Senses to connect.

Choose to focus on one or more elements of your Five Senses and expand one: Seeing, Touching, Tasting, Smelling, or Hearing.

Vision

Stand or sit still and focus on one place. Let your vision expand out to include more of your surroundings.

Stand or sit still. Stare into space. Experience your vision emanating from deep in your head.

Rotate from the waist, keeping your spine upright and relaxed and let your body swing from side to side.

Your softened eyes will move over the terrain. This will enhance your capacity to see more vividly. Be careful. If you feel dizzy, stop and rest.

Gaze at something from nature that you find beautiful. Focus your eyes on two distinct objects—for example a tree and a flower, or a rock and a blade of grass. Notice how separate each one is from the other. Each one lives within a boundary, and has shape and surface, giving it unique singularity.

Contemplate all the ways in which they invisibly join in a mutual relationship. Through sharing oxygen, creating carbon monoxide, and sharing water, one contributes to the nutrients of the other. If in close proximity, they share sunlight and rain. Their roots may mingle. They are an example of perfect autonomy and oneness existing in simultaneous mutuality. This is astonishing to contemplate: absolute autonomy, absolute connection; one serving and enhancing the other in a completely reciprocal relationship.

Taste

Relax your lips and let the breath move softly in and out of your lungs. Release yourself into your space and body. Let the air breathe you. Let your sense of taste expand with the breath and expand out of your mouth into the air around you.

Enjoy trying different tastes.

Touch

Close your eyes and let your senses reach out to whatever is there: noise, quiet, barking, water running. It is all a part of life. Expand into it. Reach out with your hand and find something to touch. Feel as if you are touching this for the first time and slowly move over it. Keep your breath open and unrestricted.

Reserve this time for some body tending. Get some lotion for a great foot massage. Pull up those tired, aching feet and slather them lavishly. Rub them as if they are the feet of a person you adore.

❦ Hearing

Focus on one thing you hear and let it dominate you. Blot out all other sounds. Try softer and quieter sounds each time. Make the switch from hearing with your ears to listening with your whole body. This will take you into a whole new creative form of 'hearing', true listening. *Hearing is the first sense to develop and the last to go at death. It is not possible to be deeply in your hearing and to also run stressed thoughts through your brain. Hearing is a way to get quickly present.*

❦ Smell

Smells surround you, some straight from the Earth and some from the world. Explore the various layers of aromas. Find and breathe in one you like and revel in it. How deeply into your body can you inhale this scent? Can you train yourself to remember the scent?

Keep a pure aroma essence on hand. The company Young Living sells therapeutic-grade essential oils which are wonderful for this. Find some essences you love.

CHAPTER FOUR
ENGAGE. INTERACT. APPRECIATE.

B reathe. Healthy breathing is a reliable route to increased health and well-being. When we breathe in fresh air, we oxygenate the blood and invite Earth and Universal energies into our body. These energies always operate in balance and bring us into the present moment. They give us a fresh perspective and organically alter our behavior. Alignment with Earth's energies through breath flow, along with the oxygenation of the brain, bring us into reciprocal balance.

In any moment, situation, or circumstance, you can stop, bring your attention to the breath, and take five or more easy inhalations and exhalations. Imagine the breath moving down into your belly and through the bottoms of your feet. Listen. This will automatically reconnect you to Earth and bring you back to your immediate physical reality, "connecting" your head and body.

How many times have you felt better after taking a break and getting some fresh air? "I NEED SOME FRESH AIR" is a familiar distress statement.

Breathe.

Breathe in and out a few times. Make it a belly breath.

Feel it in the soles of your feet, in your wiggling toes.

- ⟿ Step out on the porch.
- ⟿ Breathe.
- ⟿ Go for a brief stroll.
- ⟿ Breathe.

THE TRICKY PART

The tricky part in accepting the gift of vital balance through breath flow is bringing along the mind. The mind is generally plagued with self-absorption; in love with its own thoughts. This creates an excess, too much mental influence. Meditation that focuses on your body is a wonderful way to align with Earth's energies.

- ⟿ *Try: Sitting in a chair or on a cushion on the ground.*
  Breathe in and out for five counts.
  Notice any thoughts but let them pass by like cumulus clouds floating in the air.
  Come back to your breath over and over again.
  Feel your breath moving into your lungs. Learn to relax your chest so it is as if the breath is breathing you.
  Allow a simple minute to bring you into this state; your breath is your bridge to balance and has the power to move you away from your stress.
  Start with five minutes... and continue from there.

CHI GONG

One refined method of managing the mind's self-absorption is Chi Gong. (Also spelled Qigong.) In Chi Gong, the mind guides the body through gentle movements, which disciplines the mind and nudges it towards harmonizing with the body by aligning the breath with specific movements.

The mind becomes occupied trying to learn and keep the body on course and has to give up its stubborn fascination with self-absorbed thoughts.

The discipline of the mind is essential, and the journey into movement is never static or repetitious, and provides an engaging focus for the mind. The movements are never allowed to become routine, and one is encouraged to delve more deeply into each movement.

Chi Gong produces many beneficial results. Most significantly it draws the mind out from living only in the head and directs it into the willing body.

The body provides a needed home for the mind, since blending intuition, instinct, and learned knowledge equals great intelligence. Chi Gong is a powerful tool for bringing harmony to the mental, emotional and spiritual aspects of the body.

SIMPLE CHI GONG MOVEMENTS

Give them a whirl!

Shaking
Gently bounce in place, feet attached to the floor.
Let everything loosen.

Hands
Bring your hands up and down, elbows relaxed.
Imagine you are floating them through water.
This should be a free-flowing movement.

Body
Let the body follow by rotating gracefully from the waist.
Feel the Chi float you, sway, again as if in water.
Keep the movements comfortable.

↩ Chi Gong instructors can be found in your local area and online.

Reconnect to Earth by creating and dedicating a space just for you. This space can be roomy enough for you to dance in or the size of a thimble.

It can be surrounded by plants, in a garden, or just contain a few rocks, crystals, dried plants, or herbs. This space can be mobile, a few items placed on a makeshift altar that you carry with you wherever you go. Make it your own, and make sure you feel safe.

Dedicate this space to be your place of connection. When here, allow yourself to settle into Earth, and withdraw from the noises and demands of life. Each time you enter or come into contact with this place, strive to join with Earth. Allow yourself to just be, knowing that as you sit, lie, move, and breathe you are in Earth. Invite her in and she does the rest. Listen with your whole body.

ENGAGE, INTERACT, APPRECIATE.

This is where you show up, let go, and tune in. There is no need to try to be an improved human. Such goals of trying to be "more than" can actually interfere with your direct experience.

Use your space as a portal to Earth's energy.

↩ *Connect to Earth's resonance by giving a gift.*

↝ *Engage, be open through your five senses.*

↝ *Relieve your inner stress.*

↝ *In the spirit of reciprocity, show your gratitude.*

↝ *Give Earth something in return. This can be appreciation or a tangible, biodegradable gift...cornmeal, a flower....*

↝ *Thank her as you prepare to leave.*

↝ *Return to your space on a regular basis.*

In doing so, you will create an essential self-nurturing habit for your spirit and body.

There is no inner state more feminine than that of a woman who feels firmly connected, filled with instinctive wisdom, renewal, and spiritual inspiration.

Ellae: *"I'm the one who likes to nurture plants close to home. My space is right in my backyard. At one end, I have a private, protected garden. At the opposite end is my burgeoning vegetable garden. In between, grass has formed in a round area. Here, I sprinkle cornmeal each morning and give thanks to the day. I meditate and care for the plants and vegetables. When I travel, I bring my cornmeal with me, sprinkle it and give thanks no matter where I go."*

Mary: *"My altar at home is an eclectic mixture of items. In the center is a photo of Fajada Butte, a large rock at Chaco Canyon, New Mexico, and a candle. Both Fajada and the candle remind me to keep the flame of my life centered in Earth. I have rocks and feathers collected from various hikes, small items representing indigenous cultures I've studied, a crystal, and piece of Chinese jade.*

When I travel, I take a candle to light, and a few items in a small pouch from my home altar to keep me centered. It brings comfort to have my altar close to where I sleep."

CONNECT YOUR BODY TO YOUR SPACE

Here's a fun way to begin creating a space just for you.

Use about four yards of yarn.
Create a circle around yourself.

Feel free to make the yarn into the shape of an oval or use wavy lines, whatever feels right for you.

Sit in the middle and say aloud:
"This is my space. No one enters my space but me.
As I was cast from the creator, I was given this space.
The purpose of my life is to take every situation life
brings me and elevate my quality as a woman,
according to MY standards. I own my own
space with comfort and pleasure."

Sit in this feeling.

Take this feeling into life with you.

CHAPTER FIVE
INSTINCTIVE
WISDOM

LIVING WITH EARTH'S RESONANCE

When a woman is in concordance with Earth's resonance, she softly merges with Earth.

Earth communicates through us and gives us vital information. She especially communicates with women. This is done in the easiest of ways, through our instinctive awareness. All we need to do is remember her, pay attention to her, appreciate her, and trust ourselves.

Our connection to Earth brings vitality and timelessness. When she speaks to us, we receive an instinctual desire to preserve life.

The female connection to Earth's resonance provides the enormous gift of instinctive wisdom. This wisdom keeps life upright, safe, balanced, and moving forward. This gift is the natural intelligence of every woman.

Ellae: *"It is possible to be sensitive to Earth's messages and easily integrate them."*

When a woman takes the time to keep her connection with Earth and Earth's resonance strong, she becomes what she was meant to be: A bridge between Earth's intelligence and human endeavors.

This inner instinct becomes the guiding light that illuminates practical steps for creating and renewing reciprocal relationships in the world. Although it is rarely acknowledged, women are needed, often desperately, to do our critical part in dispensing unique wisdom and knowledge.

The Female Nature Benefits

The female nature benefits life since each woman has a unique vision that can contribute balance and success to any endeavor. She possesses a distinctive lens through which she sees the world and interprets the infinite kaleidoscope of life's possibilities.

Within each realm of these possibilities exists a woman who can make a skillful contribution through her personal perspective and manner of viewing the world. Each woman has every resource she needs to create in her own circle, big or small, an environment that nurtures life.

Carry Your Wisdom to the World

Instinctive wisdom manifests in many forms. One is when your "gut" tells you ahead of time how something will turn out. Perhaps you're familiar with this feeling. You might have honored it in some cases, and in others, remained silent. Learning to listen, give voice to, and honor your instinctive intelligence is vital. Earth gives women endurance as well as wisdom. She presents many opportunities for each woman to carry her wisdom into the world. If your voice isn't effective, then life on Earth has lost a valuable advocate.

Every voice is essential for the tapestry of life to be strong and unified. Your instinctive wisdom is Earth speaking through you in your actions and words.

Earth relies on you to speak for her. This wisdom rises from your body: It fills you and you express it. Learn to trust these instincts.

This instinctual intelligence relays accurate knowledge and contributes essential information. This knowledge is needed in the formation of relationships and world systems.

Our instincts make sure everything is in balance and nothing is excessively competitive, compromising, or destructive to life. The degree to which you doubt the vital importance of your role in this design is the degree to which Earth's voice is silenced. *You are her voice.*

SWEET LIKE HONEY

A woman's voice has the capacity to bring quiet assurance that calms the heart and teaches people how to be courageous. A woman can be a tremendous help to a man by sharing and voicing her instinctive wisdom. She can actually help him curtail his destructive side and guide him towards choices that benefit life.

A woman who is strongly rooted in her instinctive wisdom can offer incredible clarity and vision, and valiantly choose to be a creative female leader. On the other hand, when she silences her voice, she dismisses and denies her tremendous authority. She also denies loved ones the help they need. And, sadly, her own uniquely contributing voice

INSTINCTIVE WISDOM

has been stilled. As she feeds and grows her feminine capacities, her personal charisma grows. She offers a quiet assurance that invites others to believe in themselves and have the courage to speak their own creative truth. As she feeds and grows her creativity, she inspires others to develop the creative parts of themselves.

EARTH'S MESSAGES

Each woman has the ability to communicate with Earth through her body and to receive messages. The messages may be as simple as "I'd better wear a warmer jacket." Or the messages may help you comprehend that to cut the trees down will cause irreversible harm to your neighborhood.

Other examples of Earth's messages may be:

- *Getting a gut sense your loved one needs more veggies.*
- *Getting the sense your employee is struggling.*
- *Feeling compelled to run for city council, not for the power, but to speak for Earth.*
- *Starting a company that helps instead of takes.*
- *Knowing that the milk needs to be replaced even before you smell it.*
- *Sensing the plant needs to be cared for even before you feel the soil.*
- *Awaking one morning with a certainty that the chemicals coming from the factory down the road are causing health problems.*
- *Having a knowing feeling that the dogs at the Humane Society need some love and attention.*

You are life. You reproduce life. You renew life.

You know what is best because you are a part of Earth and Earth communicates through you all the time. As you learn to connect to Earth and her resonance, you will increasingly trust your instinctive wisdom. Life will benefit.

What Makes Your Body Feel Most Alive?

Your body wisdom leads you towards self-nurturing and well-being.

This encouragement to trust your body, your intuition, and your instinctive wisdom may bring up feelings of nervousness or distrust. But it is possible to prove to yourself that this wisdom resides in you. Through experimenting with the exercises below, you can learn to clarify your decisions, make choices based on what makes your body feel most alive. Start with small situations in your life. Gradually, you can build your self-trust.

Desired Fruit

Go to the produce section at your local grocery store. Pick up each piece of fruit that interests you. Sense which one your body responds to with increased vitality, a gentle strengthening. Some possible responses include feeling uplifted, warmth, or a feeling of increased strength. You may just "feel better," or lighter and joyful. Through this activity, you encourage your body to choose the desired fruit. You have made a wonderful step toward learning to trust your instinctive wisdom.

Colors and Textures

Another excellent way to tune into your body's voice is through experimenting with the colors and textures of your clothing. Color, fabric, and style have a strong influence on your body. It is fun to sense your body's reactions to various colors and enjoy the most beneficial color for you to wear on a given day.

Stand in front of your closet looking at the spectrum of colors. Pay attention to which colors draw you in. What strengthens you? What feels good? You can do the same with touch. Run your hands over a few fabric choices and check out your reaction. When you put on your outfit, don't first look in the mirror to see how it looks on you.

Look down and experience how it feels on you. You may never even get around to looking in that mirror because you feel so good. You just know it is right for you this day. If you have a wardrobe made up of a few practical colors, black for instance, you might want to consider giving your body more color choices.

The body and spirit are keenly sensitive to color, even to the point of resulting in altered feelings. Over time, turn your closet into a rainbow.

Vary the fabrics too. As your closet feeds your body's love of color and variety, your liveliness and sense of vitality will grow.

The Big Stuff

As you experiment with making small choices to act from your instinctive wisdom, move into more challenging areas of your life, the big stuff.

Let your body guide you as you learn to discern between your emotional reactivity and your body's instinctive wisdom by paying attention. Emotional reactions tend to be strong and loud, while the vital body reactions are stable and subtle.

Strong and loud emotional responses do not usually further life in the direction of mutuality and reciprocity. Emotional reactions generally move life towards excess. But your body knows what response will lead to the path of reciprocity.

For example, if a friend brings up a sore subject there are several responses you can choose. Previously, you might have chosen the response that held the strongest emotional charge for you, mistaking it for the appropriate response. Often emotionally charged reactions muddle the situation further and create chaos.

CHECK YOUR NEW ABILITIES NOW

Tune in to your body. Run through your choices. Pay attention. If your body gently strengthens on a possible response, trust the sensation. Feel free to express this response. It is likely the most beneficial reaction. A step towards resolving the conflict between you and your body has occurred, and now real communication can develop. Keep in mind that the appropriate response may be to stay quiet, take some time for yourself, and create some distance from your friend. Stay tuned into your body and stay present. When the timing is right, your instinctive wisdom will tell you when and how to approach your friend and resolve the conflict.

Ellae: "I learned this technique in the 1970s at a Gestalt therapeutic group. I was in the hot seat, trying to come to terms with an important decision about my career. I had two very distinct options: to become an employee or an entrepreneur. As I sat in my emotional quagmire, my therapist said, 'Which of these choices makes your body feel most alive?' The comparison was stunning. I immediately entered the world of the entrepreneur. Even though that decision has made my life less financially secure, it has suited my temperament perfectly and led me into extraordinary, enriching experiences. Each one had been filled with self-knowledge and dynamic relationships with others."

Your Body's Amazing Wisdom

By starting this practice in small arenas and slowly moving into the larger ones, you will build a familiarity with your own signals. You will develop a trust in yourself and your body's amazing wisdom. Reciprocal relationships will emerge.

You will learn to nurture your body, indulge your creativity, and respond to the world from your instinctive female knowing. This will feed your vitality and femininity, and keep you filled with love, warmth, and strength. You will move from one moment to the next, awash with inner comfort and confidence.

Ellae: *"Manifesting through my body is a technique I have used for a long time. I have been single for many years. Every once in a while, I think, 'It would be great to have a partner.'*

"I would follow the steps in the exercise on the next page. What floated up in front of me was my love of personal freedom. I thought deeply each time about what was more important to me: a deep and meaningful relationship or my personal freedom. Until recently, my personal freedom always won. So I would manifest something else: a successful career, male friendships, a loving relationship with my family, etc. When pursued with diligence, this technique has never failed me. We manifest what we feel."

MANIFESTING THROUGH YOUR BODY

⊕ You can manifest your dreams and visions and your body and connection to Earth can help you. The best times to manifest are in the morning when you first awaken and at night before you go to sleep.

⊕ Imagine . . . What do you want? A career change? A loving partner? To live in a house on the beach? If you can dream it, you can do it!

⊕ Let your body guide you. Feel the feelings. Allow your body to have all the feelings that you will experience when what you want has happened.

⊕ Sit in your new corner office with a magnificent view of the city. Make the executive decisions. Feel the gratitude and ability to influence.

⊕ Lie in the arms of your future spouse. Feel his or her loving embrace.

⊕ Open the French doors to your beachfront property. Feel the breeze blow your hair around in the wind.

⊕ Any feeling or belief that your body has that is opposed to what you are creating will float up in front of you.

⊕ Return to focusing your feelings on what you want.

⊕ You are manifesting your desires and dreams through your feelings.

INSTINCTIVE WISDOM

CHAPTER SIX
EARTH IS THE TEACHER

GUIDELINES FOR A WOMAN'S LIFE

Earth is the school, life is the classroom, experience is the teacher, and nature is the textbook that teaches us how to contribute harmony and happiness. The guidelines for a woman's life are woven into the fabric of nature.

Turn up the volume.

Create the intent to look, listen, and learn.

NATURE GIVES HER ALL

Flowers blossom, dew and moisture form, spiders weave intricate webs: Every aspect of nature gives her all in every moment. Never does Nature let her quality slip. We rely on her consistent commitment to quality, just as we are relied upon. Draw your inspiration from her. Then be inspirational yourself.

Let her teach you how to create harmony and sustainability in your relationships and life systems. Choose to stay aware, to listen to Earth's voice within your body. Let these lessons of the natural world elevate the quality of life within you and your circle of influence.

Your Circle of Influence

Your level of consciousness determines the quality of life you experience. You are the dominant force guiding and inspiring your everyday activities and informing the overarching reality you live in.

Even if you feel powerless in your life, you have a tremendous influence on what's around you. As a female, what you do and don't do affects the creation of life, all of life. It is important to stay aware of the reality you are creating through your thoughts, words, choices, and actions.

Reflect.

What are you putting out through your words, actions, and thoughts? How can you mimic Earth? How can you upgrade?

Earth's Gifts

Earth's gifts rearrange our current understanding of "gifting." Earth's gifts are an instinctive extension of her nature. They are given with no reason, requirement, or strings attached.

You also give gifts. These gifts are a natural extension of your unique nature.

Opportunities of the Female on a Female Planet

In a lecture, Gregge Tiffen specified that Opportunities of the Female on a Female Planet are[1]:

-Ꙩ *Reproduction*
-Ꙩ *Renewal*

---

1. See Gregge Tiffen, www.g-systems.com.

- *Adaptability*
- *Sustainability*
- *Endurance*
- *Resiliency*
- *Expansion*
- *Spiritual Renewal, and*
- *Instinctive Wisdom.*

We gain these gifts because Earth's vitality fills the cells of our bodies and in turn, we are imbued with Earth consciousness. When we are close to Earth we strengthen each one of these qualities in ourselves.

We have the right to choose how we communicate the gifts according to our personal values, ethics, and personalities. Earth has no discrimination in her gifting. She gives differently not more. Equality is part of the beauty.

Earth is the mirror for you.
Earth... guides, renews, balances, inspires.
Within her vibrates quietude and joy.
And you are the mirror of Earth.

What are the gifts that you give? What are the qualities you have that become a gift to others?

Contemplate your own wonderful, life-giving gifts, akin with Earth's, that are instinctive to your nature. Giving these gifts is not laborious or draining, but instead, the gifting fills you with a sense of purpose and connection to life. Your gifting evolves an inner appreciation of your own distinctive and worthwhile qualities. Your gifts are the same as Earth's and are also made unique by your person.

Reflect.

What are your gifts? What are the contributions you make just by being yourself?

Ask.

Ask this question of a few trusted friends. And to make it more interesting, ask someone you've had conflicts or disagreements with.

Ellae: *"I wanted everything I was to enhance others. I asked this very same question to trusted friends and to people who don't like me! Whew, I gained a new appreciation for gifting. I learned that I have enhanced the lives of others through nurturing and caring. This was great to hear.*

"But, I also learned that I can be arrogant and irritable. I listened as the individuals who don't like me attested to this. But they also said they grew through the challenge my less pleasant side had brought to them.

"I love the concept that the value of life is increased when we use every life event to enhance our personal quality."

RENEW AND REFRESH

A woman's ability to renew and refresh is legendary. Through extending small gestures of affection, generosity, and thoughtfulness to friends, family, and strangers, a woman is in-powered to shift her external world.

LOOK WITHIN

Look within and identify how you have personalized these most feminine attributes for yourself. These are the intrinsic elements of creation and thriving. Take some time to recognize that these qualities rise from within you. You have and use them constantly because they are as much a part of your nature as they are of the Earth's.

These gifts are yours and you naturally embody them. They carry your femininity, health, and slow aging. You have the absolute right to express and strengthen these characteristics. In this way, allow them to embolden your essential female nature.

CREATIVITY

Earth is creative for her own pleasure and the outgrowth of her pleasure is life, balanced and beautiful. When we create for our own pleasure, we too craft a balanced and beautiful life.

Engaging in an activity you find creative nourishes and replenishes your body so it can reliably support you. This activity is a time for filling up with art, music, walking, cooking, writing business plans, dancing, carpentry—the list can be huge! Continually add to it according to your unique and expanding tastes.

Return to this list when you feel overextended. For some mysterious reason, when we feel most challenged by life, we have difficulty remembering what it takes to return to an inner sense of quiet and joyful well-being.

TRUSTING RELATIONSHIPS WITH WOMEN

Trusting relationships with other women can return us to our strength.

Ellae: "*I can be seriously stressed, talk to a dear female friend, and feel better in thirty seconds.*"

Each woman offers unique contributions to life and our lives. If we recognize and encourage one another to shine, earth and life will benefit. We believe that right now the world needs a communion of women, a force of wisdom and connectivity to get our planet and our geopolitical affairs back on track. If this resonates with you, observe your own behavior.

Ellae: "*I live in an area of Earth that is fantastically beautiful. The other day I stood on a hill side and relished the impossibly perfect foothills, gently blanketed with soft, low-lying clouds. The sun streamed down through a crisp spring breeze . . . I softly said, 'Hello, Gorgeous.' I was drenched in the recognition that I was simultaneously witnessing this exquisiteness and feeling as if my cells were being infused with loveliness.*

"*It occurred to me that I had been connecting to the beauty of nature because I felt it enhanced me as a woman. Then I made the switch to forgetting about how it enhanced me . . . and I felt the different qualities of Earth moving through me: the waterfalls, the rocks, the fog. The difference was lovely. I knew that past moment from my rest in the soybeans, comfort, connection, and gentle sweetness . . . deep pleasure.*

"*The moving grace of the waterfall is ours. The mystery of the fog is ours. The exquisiteness of being cleared by a wind when emotions are running high is ours.*

"*The phenomenon of pebble rings expanding from a tossed stone into a still and clear lake is ours. Like a flock of birds all moving in perfect unison, we have the ability to move in perfect unison with Earth and one another.*

"When I remember my connection to Earth, I am inspired. Her ability to create, reproduce, endure, and restore are also mine. Her ability to maintain perfect balance through constant reciprocity is mine and yours. So I say, 'Hello, Gorgeous' to Earth, to myself, and to each and every woman."

Become a Female Connected to Earth

Immerse yourself in Earth's resonance. Connect in. Expand. Upgrade who you are, from the inside out. Share your natural, life-giving gifts with the world. Create: For your own pleasure. Appreciate the beauty of Earth in other women. You will become as fresh and inspirational as Earth. You have the power to inspire.

Let yourself shine.

Let yourself glow like a candle in a dark room.

CHAPTER SEVEN

THE MASCULINE
& THE FEMININE

PREFACING THE CONVERSATION

We, the authors of this book, have been challenged by the chapters that deal with male and female relationships. We wanted this to be an inclusive conversation, one that is flexible and relatable. But we were well aware that the conversation could not, and would not be balanced because two women were trying to have a conversation about men and women/ the feminine and the masculine. Ellae found a wonderful Wall Street Journal article in April 2010 written by Jeffrey Zaslow titled "Friendship for Guys (No Tears!)."

We emailed Mr. Zaslow, and he happily gave us permission to quote his article in the book. So although the conversation isn't truly balanced, we have tried to weave in elements of the male experience directly from a male source.

Additionally, in this book we speak in terms of the male and female, heterosexual relationship paradigm. This isn't meant to disregard the Gay, Lesbian, Bisexual, Transgender, Queer (GLBTQ) community. We invite members of the GLBTQ

*community to receive this information and adjust it to fit their
personal lifestyle and attraction patterns.*

*Our intention in writing this is to help readers locate and
identify the male and female elements of themselves and their
personal relationships. Through a consciousness of these primal
elements of ourselves, we can use this increased knowledge to
benefit all of life in our own unique way.*

*In the end, this chapter is written by women, for women. We
invite everyone to read the book and to share their feedback on
our website: www.earthisyoursweetspot.com.*

Everything on Earth has a role to play in the ongoing evolution of life. Each living being fulfills a purpose in the plan and
male-female relationships are a central part of this design.

Our Bodies

A woman's body—and the feminine side of a man—nurtures life. The feminine seeks to create and benefit life in all
realms. The most amazing manifestation of this is our opportunity for reproduction.

In nature, reproduction comes through a female body.
Reproduction is a unique opportunity for women. Each
woman should be able to choose how or if she wants to use
this reproductive capacity and responsibility. Some women
choose to create the miracle of life after the catalytic union
with a man. Women who aren't able to reproduce in their
own body can be helped though a body of another woman.
In the midst of this elegant balance we find the capacity to
reproduce. It all works.

The feminine feels truth instinctively, often in the body,
or in "the gut," commonly called a "woman's intuition."

The male body, and the male side of a woman, protects life. The masculine side gains knowledge through observation. The masculine utilizes the information gained through observation. The unique shaping of these perceptions morphs into his ability to build systems of understanding as his contribution to life. These systems include: banking, medicine, religion, technology, warfare, science, etc. These are the systems that shape our modern day lives. Historically, men have built the systems, therefore men understand them, and they can function comfortably within them.

Now of course, there are female architects, pilots, politicians, CEOs and much more. Men and women are evolving characteristics once dominant in the other gender and this is a beautiful process. But typically, "the body rules," and men deal with issues surrounding their ability to protect life while women, on the other hand, tend to deal with issues surrounding their concerns with creating, thriving and nurturing life.

MEN AND WOMEN: REARING AND DEVELOPING

Men and women have clear, inborn differences. From early development these differences are evident. Little boys generally learn about the world through exploration, testing, challenging. This is an information gathering process. They tend to play with building blocks, learn about cars, and take things apart in order to understand how they work. Some particularly physical boys appear to bounce off of everything around them and learn through the contact.

Little girls tend to be relational, like Earth. They are more inclined to express feelings, play house, have tea parties, play with dolls, and fantasize about who they are going to marry, help one another with their feelings and demonstrate relatedness in action. Everything in nature is connected and in relationship. Everything is in constant balance and rebalance all the time. Earth is relational and girls express this naturally. A direct offshoot of their inborn connection.

If a boy has a strong feminine side, he will incline towards more relational behavior. The same is true for girls with a strong masculine side. They will incline towards systems-oriented play.

But humans are in male and female bodies, and in the end, as we just noted: the bodies will rule. The girls will be working with issues of human relating and connecting, and the boys will be working out issues having to do with building systems.

ADOLESCENCE

As we mature, these two variations typically grow more distinct. In adolescence girls begin to feel their reproductive power, and immaturely compete over body parts, popularity, and social position. At this stage of development, young women can experience challenges in their relationships with friends and family members. Girls in this age category often walk through life like caged wildcats, sharpening their claws on others.

Boys begin to experience the very basic and compelling realization that they need sex.

ADULTHOOD

These tendencies follow men and women into adulthood, and once again, "the bodies tend to rule." Women often work with issues of human relating and connecting, while men work with issues having to do with building systems.

MALE AND FEMALE FRIENDSHIPS

In Mr. Zaslow's *Wall Street Journal* article, he discusses the differences between male friendships with other males and female friendships with other females. Male friendships are "side-by-side." Men spend valuable time together, typically around an event or activity, like playing poker or watching sports.

"What they don't do is sit around as a group the way women do sharing their deepest feelings," Zaslow observes. Female friendships, on the other hand, he notes, are "face-to-face. [Women] talk, cry together, share secrets."

Zaslow shares a humorous piece of commentary on female friendships:

"[Though] I envy women's easy intimacy, I also know it wouldn't work for me and my friends. I've played poker with the same guys every Thursday night for 18 years. We rarely talk about our lives. We talk about cards, betting, bluffing. I used to say that my poker buddies don't even know my kids' names.

"But then I wondered if I was exaggerating. So one night I turned to my left at the poker table and casually asked my friend Lance: 'Hey Lance, could you name my children?' He shrugged, paused to think, then smiled sheepishly. 'I could rename them,' he said.

"Men still obtain great satisfaction from their friendships, but they don't tend to expose their inner vulnerability to one another. In the words of a man from New Jersey, 'As men, we feel the need to camouflage our sensitivity. . . but that doesn't mean we're not sensitive.'"

Instead, according to the *WSJ* article, men choose to share their more "sensitive" parts with female friends, girlfriends, and wives.

Zaslow makes an interesting comment, "[Men] rarely discuss serious issues.... [They] assume [their] male friends will be of little help."

The relational orientation combined with the instinctive wisdom of women provides a safe place for us all, men, children, and other women to be vulnerable and have experiences framed in wise understanding. One of the men interviewed for the article said it best, "I wouldn't talk about my insecurities with the guys. All my real insecurities—about work, finances, the kids—those I share with my wife."

Men tend to be observational and learn through physical contact. Therefore when men interact with one another, they observe and participate in activities instead of delving into emotional issues. Women are generally more "relational," and connect through talking and sharing their experiences. When a man is with a woman, and he feels safe, he will let his guard down and expose his sensitive parts. A woman who opens to a man and becomes vulnerable too, often has first valued his successful skill in life. She then feels safer in her vulnerablilty. This can increase the personal confidence in them both.

Ellae: "A while ago, I was quite depressed and upset. Clearly off balance. I had done my Earth thing. I had done it again, and again. I was still way emotional. A dear male friend, who lives his life in a way I love, took one look at me, bought me a chocolate bar, and sat quietly while I wolfed it down. 'Better?' he said. 'Yep,' I answered. Then I thanked him for being one of the men who knows how to make women happy. A happy woman makes life better for everyone. Earth's intention is for men and women to balance each other out. So how do we get into such confusion over how to do that?"

MALE AND FEMALE RELATIONSHIPS AND ADULT SEXUALITY

To be an adult male is a little like living in a room without windows. Men often feel a sense of isolation. Since early childhood, a man builds a worldview based on perceptions of what he observes, participates in, and the outcome of the experience.

The perceptions gained from this allow him to develop a system of understanding that is uniquely his. It is a structure of concepts, and one perception justifies and generates another, like something built with blocks. To know a man, you need to understand his system for making sense of life.

> I look at my life as a box . . . So everything that I put in—learn how to play guitar, put that in the box. The friends I made, I put that in the box, and my career grew. Everything around me—all of the awards and all of the songs I wrote and all the success and everything put that in that box. That box built and grew into this wonderful house. (Kenny Chesney on "Oprah," April 2010).

The stability of this structure is a comfort zone for many men and it explains the sense of isolation men can feel.

Women have a tendency to live and dwell in connection and emotion, and again, their brain chemistry reflects this.

A man tends to be alone and observes life from his room. Each woman he comes into contact with provides a window, an opening through which he can join into her comfort, warmth, and connection. The woman, the host, receives him. He is the guest. She isn't looking out a window, because she is already outside, immersed in nature. She wants company.

She desires to enhance her pleasure by being joined. He enhances his pleasure by feeling connected.

HE IS IN THE CONNECTION

When a man is close to a woman emotionally, but primarily sexually, he leaves his sense of being contained. He moves out through the window that has opened to him, the receptive woman. He gets to connect instead of observe. When he makes love to a woman, he is in the connection, feasting on it. Each woman in her unique loveliness offers a different stimulation in nature's sensuousness.

The closeness of being inside of a woman's body offers a man focused passion and release. He is immersed in an enormous presence and generosity. His partner's body is merging with Earth, and so is he for those precious moments.

A sexually refined man is able to establish rewarding connections with women intellectually, emotionally, and spiritually without always longing for physical contact.

THE BIG O!

One of the few times a man relaxes is after orgasmic release. The connection a man feels inside of a woman's body allows him to give the gift of himself so deeply and in that moment he feels embraced in the feminine, completely accepted and safe. This allows for tremendous tranquility.

If a man and a woman orgasm together, a deeper capacity for compatibility and intimacy is born from the profound impact of perfectly synchronized timing in their sexual union.

Ellae: "A plain-speaking male friend of mine says simply, 'This is when you feel really good about each other.'"

AN ASPECT OF HER NATURE

A man is drawn to a woman because he is attracted to something about her. He may be purely attracted to her body parts; but in an attraction with depth, he is attracted to a specific aspect of her nature, often a part that she has not yet explored. As the connection deepens, the woman learns more about herself. Sometimes she likes what she learns and sometimes she doesn't. But it is all her. A man is precious to a woman because he brings her into more self-awareness. A woman is precious to a man because she offers him a way out of his aloneness, which in some cases even becomes isolation. She helps him make sense of his role in life.

HEALING

It feels wonderful to live in a female body unless we have gone through abuse. Abuse hurts and isolates, which is the antithesis of nature. When we feel isolated we cannot nurture ourselves. When we reconnect to Earth through our physical bodies, we begin to heal. Connection and the pleasure of belonging replace the pain. If you are healing from abuse, start by connecting with nature and her animals. You will feel less and less isolated through the inclusion and acceptance. As you strengthen, expand into connecting with humans.

Because abuse is destructive and so common, professional help is available, and often needed, to really finish the challenge and move on to be the woman you want to be.

ATTRACTION

In many relationships, a man becomes attracted to a woman and she acknowledges the attraction. If the attraction is mutual, she may draw herself closer to him. The woman may then respond to him by strengthening, often unconsciously, the parts of herself that he is relating to. Conversely, if a woman is already in conscious recognition of the part of herself that he is attracted to, she may turn him away.

Often, in a strong attraction between a man and a woman, they both want to know this part of her better. The man needs contact with this part of the woman so she can frame his life experience for him.

She needs the self-awareness, so she encourages him. The woman will come to understand she is in charge. As he explores her nature, she learns new things about herself.

Through a man, a woman can unearth essential parts of herself. A man can show a woman who she is, and it is up to her to integrate the information. A woman can choose which parts of herself she wants to expand.

Ellae: "We all know this self-awareness is not always pleasant. If we get jealous, it is something inside of us that the man is bringing up. It isn't the guy's fault. In order to come into our full radiance as women we need to know all parts of ourselves. Guys are great for getting us there. They bring our basic humanness right to the surface; our fears, vulnerabilities, strengths, deepest longings. When we are fully human, we can really evolve."

A Mature Man

A mature man understands that the woman he is with is all he needs for his connection. A mature man chooses a woman who is enough for him. He can allow her to become the center of his life. A man who chooses a woman for control-motivated issues—for instance, body parts or youth—may be unwilling or unable to experience the full wealth that a woman has to offer him. He may not be ready to be fully vulnerable, seen, and met by his partner.

In many successful long-term relationships, the areas a man explores within a woman creatively challenge her and nudge her towards inner stability and evolution. She in turn has a sustained love, interest, and encouragement in him and his life pursuits.

Her Instinctive Wisdom

Men all seek the same things: comfort, connection, and renewal from a woman's body. A great partner seeks her instinctive wisdom, intelligence and spirituality.

If the relationship works for a man, the access he receives to his partner has far-reaching effects. Her instinctive wisdom enables him to become more effective in the systems he builds in life. It takes a secure man to tolerate this level of vulnerability.

Ellae: "*A man needs a woman to be present with him and to listen to his difficulties and struggles. From there, he values the words and inspiration she offers him. This support lifts him out of his fears of inadequacy. She frames his experiences and guides him to be creative in life.*"

Are you a Creator?

Earth is a creator and a destroyer in terms of the figure eight and generates reciprocity and balance. Men and women are creative beings but also have a capacity for destruction.

Men most often work with forms of power, authority, and hierarchy. A man who is caught in his destructive patterns can attempt to manipulate or move a system towards an outcome he desires. This can create a tendency to control, to take away free will from another. And as a result, he can build systems that harm life.

Certainly not all aggression is simply destructive, much of it is protective. If a man finds out that his wife has been wronged or hurt, he may become enraged. This aggression is deeply rooted in his love for his wife and his desire to protect her. This fusion of aggression and protection can be a hard one to keep nondestructive for a man.

A woman who is caught in her destructive patterns can devour just as nature does. This dance of destruction and devouring is tremendously negative. Devouring comes when our sense of connection turns dark, our sense of self-reliance corrodes, and we become greatly dependent on others. A destructive woman devours much like the mother cat that eats her kittens to keep them safe.

The root of this devouring is the need for safety and inclusion. A strong connection to Earth can balance this devouring behavior, and replace it with a capacity to strengthen personal boundaries. It is interesting and important to ask yourself "Am I a creator, or a destroyer? And what is my trigger?" Aim to ask the question without self-criticism or judgment: Take an honest look at your life, your choices, and your current reality.

Ꝙ Do a gentle check-in, and pay attention to:
↝ When you are caught in old patterns.
↝ When you cultivate a new response.

THE RESULTS

Are you living the results you want? Do you actively take part in the creation of self-honesty, love, beauty, reciprocal relationships, and the pursuit of your passions? If the answer is, "no," begin to imagine your life as a blank slate, a new page for you to fill up with creation. One step at a time is just the right pace.

If you destroy something, or life takes something away, you can rebuild something from the rubble, or even play in the rubble of crumbled expectations.

IS HE A CREATOR?

It is also valuable to ponder your friendships and personal relationships. If you have a man in your life, you can ask yourself the same question of him, "Is he primarily a creator, or a destroyer?" When human beings are afraid, they make destructive choices, often born from the desire to control an outcome. A woman who is actively tuning into Earth and her resonance, and nurturing Earth as her primary relationship is inspired to create.

Such a woman can also inspire the people around her and the men in her life.

MEN AND WOMEN—ARCHETYPAL FEARS

The archetypal fear of many women is to be rejected. In nature everything transforms into something else. A mother bird rejects a defective baby and the baby dies....yes. But the baby's body is incorporated into the soil, the air, and creates life in other ways. The baby doesn't get rejected from Nature. It has changed. Earth is reciprocal. She uses everything, nothing is wasted. All is grist for the mill. Nothing ever really ends, it transforms into something else.

When a woman experiences rejection in a relationship, she can get an excruciating jolt. Unless she can see how to transform the experience, she hurts. If it is a true ending it is even worse. If a woman has not developed and nurtured a strong relationship with Earth, this jolt can be especially strong because she has no place to retreat for strength and then direct an experience of continuity. A woman who has a broken heart will feel resilient if she can create continuity of some sort for herself . . . Tending, enjoying, and journeying into nature is always a help. The very connectedness is healing. It is at these times the connection to nature can seem the most miraculous, inspiring the needed transformation.

The archetypal fear of many men is inadequacy. This is because the male "systemizing brain" gathers information and builds systems. When a man materializes success in these realms, a feeling of internal adequacy is often born. However, when a man feels compromised in this role he can become driven by his fears of inadequacy. Men often long to leave their mark. To be remembered for an achievement, a contribution. It is a wonderful longing and deserves to be supported by women.

Wonderful men drive to protect; they serve as providers. In many cultures men have acted as financial providers. As banks, stock markets, religious institutions, and other global systems are breaking, both men and women are finding it challenging to function. Many people feel lost, unclear, or afraid.

This may be especially difficult, nuanced, and frightening for men because they are struggling to serve their role as protectors. Some men may experience feelings of helplessness and desperation, and resort to negative self-talk. This vulnerability provides an opportunity for women to be critical and cruel. Now, more than ever, it is vital for a woman to avoid making men feel inadequate. Instead, she can use her resiliency, instinctive wisdom, strength and kindness to inspire courage.

Relationship Challenges

When a relationship turns negative, either party may unconsciously or consciously play into their partner's archetypal fear. In this scenario, a woman disempowers a man by triggering his fear of inadequacy; the man then delivers a rejecting statement or action.

For example, a woman may say, "I am miserable because of you." The man may then tell her, "I can't take you anymore. I'm leaving."

If the destructive scenario is allowed to develop, a messy cycle spirals out of control, eventually creating a war zone. If the relationship does not improve, both parties should consider seeking professional help.

Ellae: "Many of the conversations women have with one another about men revolve around discussing a man's inadequacy. To transform relationships with men in all walks of our lives, this behavior needs to be rooted out like a noxious weed. Through our choices, words, and actions we can develop a language of appreciation that replaces the old fault finding. Instead of criticizing, we can gently guide and appreciate a man's efforts with smiles and gratitude. These simple, new responses and behaviors create an environment of willingness, support, and cooperation. You are the woman, you are the center, you are in control. It starts with you."

A MAN IN LOVE

Any man in love has only one wish: to please the woman he loves. When a woman who is dissatisfied with her man resorts to hurting him through his fear of inadequacy, he might feel useless to her. This can be both devastating to the man, and to the relationship. Some men may respond with aggression in order to protect themselves.

Sadly, some men who have experienced sentiments of inadequacy refuse to open themselves up to a woman ever again. They cannot allow themselves to be vulnerable. Instead, they withdraw, and walk around, love phobic. We then lose the protective interactions of kind and loving men.

A woman needs to be conscious of her words, deeds, and actions, in order to avoid causing too much harm.

CLEAR COMMUNICATION

Every woman must find clear ways to communicate with the men in her life—her father, sons, mates, brothers, friends, bosses, or employees. This means using words that give information, but do not blame. Through maintaining a direct connection to Earth, a woman can develop gentle, accepting, and clear communication with men.

Earth inspires the personal strength that underlies this type of communication.

CHAPTER EIGHT
FEMALE POWER

As we stated earlier in this book, as a woman you have an enormous degree of power in your personal sphere of influence. Unfortunately, many women are not aware of their own significance, or of the imprint they are making in the interconnected matrix of life.

By observing nature's intricate and reciprocal balance, a woman can learn about her own strength. Nature provides a constant metaphor: A small, gurgling river flows for miles and finally meets the breaking waves of the ocean. As a woman chooses to remember her connection to Earth, she may naturally awaken to her own power and join others in her impact for change.

Ellae: *"Don't pretend you have no power in your world, or that you have limited power. You are tremendously powerful. You are a woman connected to Earth."*

Remember:

- Mount St. Helens eruption created a new influx of life so rapidly that even the most educated scientists were stunned at the speed of the regeneration.

- Eleanor Roosevelt is said to have remarked, "A woman is like a tea bag. You don't know what she is capable of until she is in hot water."

- A lily emerges in solitary splendor in the garden. Enhancing the beauty of every other plant by its presence.

*"In every woman there is a queen.
Speak to the Queen, and the Queen will answer."*
NORWEGIAN PROVERB

FEMININITY AND RELATIONSHIPS

Ellae: "*It is important for a woman to maintain her personal power and confident leadership in relationships. If a woman gives her power to a man, he will take it and he won't give it back. A woman has to pull it back and that can be difficult for her as well as threatening to the man.*

"There are many forces in our lives that take our energy, including our families, taxing jobs, philanthropic work, and friends. Even if you get enormous pleasure back, you may find you have nothing left to give. You may be exhausted. It takes far too much energy to retrieve your power once it is parceled out. This may seem to be the price one pays for a deeply committed life. You can pull your vitality back with varying amounts of effort or you can stay connected to nature and just simply not get depleted."

Think About...

Here are a few things to think about and gently pay attention to in the dynamics of female power and relationships:

- Do you use men as entertainment? Through fantasy, male bashing, excessive discourse with friends? If so, are you just distracting yourself from some thing more important that needs your attention? Your own self-knowledge perhaps?

- Do you believe a man or a relationship can solve your problems?

- Have you contemplated giving up your career to be supported by a significant other, forgetting the importance of reciprocity?

> *"The worst thing a woman can do is to become financially dependent on a man."*
> GREGGE TIFFEN

- Do you swagger your nature or squash and silence who you are to impress others, or to please a man?

If you are currently struggling with some of the issues posed in the questions above, or you have struggled with them in the past, it is okay. Just acknowledge it, notice the results, and decide if you want to change or not.

A WOMAN'S RESPONSIBILITY

It is a woman's responsibility to retain her power. She can choose to enhance her awesome femininity instead of becoming lost in or dependent upon others, especially a man. A woman radiates strength and vibrancy when her femininity and instinctive wisdom become the center of her life. To be well connected to Earth means being in the loving pleasure of our bodies. When your body is filled with this pleasure, stress is not present.

In Western cultures, most people don't nurture a warm and loving relationship with Earth. As a result, we become distracted away from our warm and loving relationship with nature through our bodies. But we long for that feeling, and we begin to look for sources of pleasure outside of ourselves instead of recognizing that we are the source. For this reason, many women seek to connect to their bodies by making love to attain this birthright. This is a wonderful way to connect into our luxurious female bodies. But this can cause a woman to rely on being desired and the sexual experience as a source of both Earth and the sensation of pleasure inside her body.

Many women rely on their sexual partners to get them into their bodies, and experience this sensation of pleasure. This can cause a host of imbalanced, unhealthy, or painful experiences to emerge for a sexually active woman. After sex, a woman experiences a feeling of rightness that lasts three or four days. But it begins to wane, and if a woman does not return to Earth and nurture a strong relationship with nature, she will hunger for the man and turn towards him for aspects of support.

The need, or demand, can create discomfort or unease for the man and further his desire to create distance.

Thankfully we are what we are looking for. This completeness is in us already, and we can return to the connection at any time. The gift of this pleasure and love is us.

The man has only allowed the woman to remember who she is. He is not the reason she got there.

Ellae: *"Having fabulous sex and releasing into Earth is an incredible combination. When you completely immerse into Earth, and share it with a partner, it is stunning. I remember a wonderful sexual experience. I was lying in bed afterwards, complete, full, in total rightness, needing nothing more. My partner whispered, 'When can we do it again?'*

I am the fountain. I am the source. So are you."

A Woman's Sexual Power

Women personally experience, and then share, potent female power when engaging in sexual intercourse. Women have sex for many reasons. For an immature woman, sex can be about competition and winning. For a mature woman who is involved in non-exploitative sex, it is about sensuality, pleasure, connection, beauty, relationship, giving and receiving in reciprocity, vitality, the profound pleasure of deep, surrendered release, and love.

These are all the sensuous qualities of a strong connection to Earth. When a woman nurtures her connection to Earth through her female body, she may feel the resonance of an orgasm pulsing lightly within her all the time. This is an affirmation of her essential relationship. Non-exploitative sex is about returning and reconnecting to Earth, and retaining this connection.

The great sexual partners relish us as we lead the way back to Earth.

A message to young women....

"The most powerful person in the world is a beautiful young woman."

(Source unknown)

A young woman in a brand spanking new body is in a unique period when she has so much power, but often she doesn't know how to handle it. Each woman has the beautiful responsibility to accept her sexual self. We are surrounded by sex-stimulation. When these external forces are combined with healthy hormones, the drive can be intense. Deep and driving feelings that may not be tempered by maturity can emerge. A myriad of repercussions, like unplanned pregnancies, venereal diseases, and jaded feelings about sex, can explode upon the scene. If a young woman does not learn to harmonize with her sexuality, distrust for men can come forward early, and never be completely resolved.

The gift of sex is a tremendous power and this power needs to be wisely guided at all times. Older women need to be effective mentors and older men wise protectors.

 Reflect.

Take a moment and reflect on how you can become quietly rooted in your own strength. Let your body and your connection to Earth guide you to your true nature. A woman in her nature is naturally confident.

Ellae: "When a woman is in her true nature, it is heart-stoppingly exquisite. I was not born to this way of being. I have been lucky enough to have great friends and teachers who have shown this path to me. Before I was 'aware', I would occasionally notice a woman who just took my breath away. It had nothing to do with Madison Avenue beauty. It was a mysterious something else.

"I remember being at a lecture and the woman behind me had this quality, this elusive exquisite quality. I started up a conversation and she confided in me that many men had told

her she was essentially feminine. She was like the fresh breeze, a warm ray of sunlight, a nourishment flowed from her. She was a nurse and she lived in her garden surrounded by her plants and animals. I now know that each one of us can be perfectly feminine in our own mold."

   Connect to Earth. Choose how you want to express your femininity and then claim it. Be it with confidence and leadership.

Remember your Femininity

Be tender with yourself: Personal growth is a process.

Return your attention back on you. Nurture yourself.

Take a hot bath, massage the wonderful feet that carry you through the day.

Take a walk, engage and breathe deeply.

Are you troubled by a problem? Use your vision to invite communication and see if an answer comes through nature.

Delve into your creativity.

Do the most nurturing thing you can do for yourself.

Call a dear woman friend and laugh together.

Create beauty.

Express yourself with greater eloquence.

Own your courage.

Understand the saying "In the ugliest of life beauty still bubbles up." Notice it. Appreciate it. Engage it.

Self-nurturing also has to do with seeing and interacting with whatever is in your sphere this moment. The green leaves on the trees. They are there for others, and they are there for you to nurture yourself with. Simply resonate with their beauty. Marvel at each moment . . . Embrace her using your five senses and merge.

Remember Who You Truly Are

Remember your femininity and become strongly rooted in it through self acknowledgement actualized into action. Over time, as you engage Earth, remember who you truly are. You can move through life with your femininity as your beacon. You will glow like a candle in a dark room.

To Be Pleased by a Man

A woman should only pick a man who truly pleases her. A man who is happy with his work, a man who is not competitive with her success, and a man who protects instead of excessively controlling. His capacity in these realms should suit her so that she has no need to criticize him.

This is only possible if she picks him because of a deep connection, not one solely based on body parts, good looks, or wealth. She also needs to seek a man who has the desire to cherish her instinctive wisdom and then use it to enhance his information gathering. These qualities provide strong cornerstones for love to emerge and grow.

A mature man loves the woman he is with for her instinctive wisdom. A man needs to pick a woman who he feels accepted by, and a woman to whom he is fully satisfying. Her unique generosity must suit his needs. He shouldn't feel as if he constantly needs to prove himself. He should find her a comfort to be with, filled with warmth and wisdom that he finds useful so that fear of inadequacy is not present. In choosing a partner from these wise vantage points, strong emotional bonds are forged.

This is especially true when the love both partners share for the woman's body becomes the center of the relationship.

How do I know if he "truly pleases me?"

This, too, is very personal. Only you know. Your ability to choose the right guy depends on your level of self-knowledge. In every situation, seek to know yourself better.

But there are some guidelines to assist you in your decision as you make progress in increasing your self-knowledge.

- ⇨ *Is he happy with his work and the contribution he is making?*
- ⇨ *Does appreciate and value you?*
- ⇨ *Does he know how to nurture and drink kindly from the fountain—you—that he draws from?*
- ⇨ *Is he non-competitive with you about your success?*
- ⇨ *Does he encourage you in your life pursuits?*
- ⇨ *Does he successfully channel his temper?*
- ⇨ *Does he seek and respect your wisdom, and how you frame life?*
- ⇨ *Does he love and challenge you to evolve in the ways you long to grow?*
- ⇨ *Does he make you laugh? A happy woman makes life happier.*
- ⇨ *Is he able to trust you, or does he excessively control you?*

Create a list of your own:

According to your own self-knowledge, write down what you think is important for your personal partner. Feel free to get a fresh sheet of paper if you need more space.

1. _____

2. _____

3. _____

Your job is to find a way to communicate with the man in your life that is gentle and clear, so that you don't criticize. Give up trying to control him by criticizing. When women criticize, men feel inadequate. This may cause his shadow or destructive side to come up.

LOVE

As we mentioned earlier, when a man and a woman are deeply in love, the only thing a man wants is to be enough for his woman. He wants nothing more than to please her. This is so important for a woman to realize. He wants to please her and is afraid he will be inadequate, which makes him pretty vulnerable.

Appreciate him!

CHANGE

Women and men frequently respond to change in different ways. A woman often changes when it is necessary to create and flourish in life.

As we stated earlier, men have "systemizing" brains and tend to build their beliefs around them like a structure. If a man falls in love, his feelings for the woman introduce the need to expand and change. This can be very scary for a man because change and expansion mean destabilizing his structure.

This can be a very crucial turning point in a relationship. This is a time when he may express to her, sometimes in a tender moment, how his destructive side may come into action.

For example, he may tell her in the simplest of terms, usually looking away, "I am unreliable." "I am a player." "I threw the baby out with the bathwater." " I have a drug problem." "I say one thing and do another."

This vulnerable statement is a gift, and these words should be taken seriously.

If this occurs, it is important for the woman to contemplate the warning. This is his destructive behavior. Can she handle it? She can ask herself, "Is this an opportunity for growth and learning I want? Do I choose this?" Most significantly, a woman can decide if she can accept the light and dark elements of him and his behaviors. She can evaluate whether she can manage the relationship in the long term without making him feel inadequate.

And does she have the courage to do the same?

These revelations are essential turning points in a relationship. The other partner can stop, deliberate, and decide if they want to let this person into their world or move on. The woman in particular can use this as an opportunity to tap into her instinctive wisdom. She can determine whether she wants to share her body with this man, and whether she should make herself vulnerable to his destructive side.

Women and Change

When a woman is emotionally hurt, Earth offers a metaphor for healing that many women understand naturally. For example, when a toxic substance is poured upon nature, all the plants and wildlife show the trauma by dying. It appears to onlookers that dead is the whole story, but Earth has the ability to take whatever insult she is given and bring new life. The dead state is creatively transformed.

Nature has adapted, evolved, and generated a new form. When a woman has been emotionally hurt, she frequently withdraws. When she turns inside of herself, she has the potential to generate a state of internal healing. New life can be formed from this toxic experience. She reaches into her fertile inner terrain and recognizes the beneficial elements of the experience. This doesn't mean the experience is right or defensible: The experience may have been very wrong. The personal work may be very hard, but like Earth, any woman has the capacity to heal from within. The new life she brings up can be new evolutions of herself.

Having this great regenerating capacity means no woman needs be a victim forever. An essentially feminine woman utilizes a wounding experience and becomes a higher quality person according to her own personal standards. All is fertilizer for new life. The gift of this refinement is grace.

The Art of Reciprocity

Reciprocal relating is a wonderful skill to apply in these situations. It brings our creative reactions and responses to life. Give only as much nurturing as is received and withdraw from giving more than is in balance. Reciprocity flourishes life. A woman may not like a wounding experience, but she can honor it and use it to become a better woman. Without the man touching into her so deeply, she would never have discovered this area that needed to be strengthened and upgraded.

A woman never needs to be a victim. She has the ability, just like Earth, to bring up new life from every experience. She has a choice in every situation and relationship in her life to enhance her loveliness and sensuality, and to create behaviors and outcomes that are new. Any response to being hurt that does not create a new reaction within oneself is repetitious and does not increase self-knowledge.

Femininity comes from being alive to the constant truth that every situation can birth a new, beautiful experience. Even though some experiences make us dig deep, particularly the abusive ones, the opportunity for healing is always present. The healing occurs when a woman has seen how she has become a better person, through her own efforts, as a result of the experience. She can then honor herself and her creative ability. It doesn't make the experience right. It may have been very wrong, but she has triumphed and become more female. She must honor the experience for the courage and strength she has found. This strengthens her gentle female essence.

Find an Opportunity to Heal

Take three minutes and free write about a past or current relationship with a significant other.

- ❖ Were you hurt or did you do the hurting?
- ❖ Do you still carry the wound?

↪ How does it feel?

  ↪ What color is it?

    ↪ Where in your body do you feel the wound?

      ↪ Do you want to offer reciprocal relating to the experience?

Go for a walk.

With Earth.

Connect in.

Look for advice in nature.

Let go.

Just be.

You can make another choice.

Have the courage to make your best
   attempt at reciprocity.

FIND YOUR COMPATIBLE PARTNER

This is an exercise for a woman who is looking for a compatible partner and is based on the concept of balanced opposites: Attracting a partner who is your synergistic partner.

Get a piece of paper. On the left side, write down all of your characteristics.

You may need to talk to friends and family members so that you aren't being too soft, or too hard, on yourself. This should be a balanced representation of who you are as a person. When that list is complete, sit with it, and add anything new that occurs to you.

On the right side, write down each one of the characteristics that you feel would be your balanced opposite. This is entirely personal.

Two Examples of Opposites

If you are quiet, your balanced opposite might be passionate, energetic, or humorous. If you are a businesswoman, you might find that your balanced opposite is a highly successful scientist, a violinist, or even an Italian wine grower. Only you know or can discover this answer. You are sculpting your partner.

This process increases your self-knowledge. Now read aloud what you have written. Sound is the first step in manifestation. Then feel the "body feelings" that will emerge when you have this partner.

The partner will come. Surrender timing to the universe.

You can revisit this piece of paper often, or just once. Have the courage to live your longing.

CHAPTER NINE

IT'S ALL ABOUT YOU

For a woman, coming to terms with her sexual self is often her first great task. The choices she makes will affect the rest of her life.

THE ENTRANCE

A woman has the power and the absolute right to choose how to open to men in her life. The woman has the right and responsibility to control the entrance. When a woman chooses to open, she can receive what the man has to offer and has the opportunity to give those parts of herself that she desires to share. She can then deeply enhance her self-knowledge by taking the time to integrate the impact of the man's presence on her life.

If, after this experience, she is displeased, it is important that she evaluate whether she should open to him again. It is possible that she may choose that the experience was useless, repetitious, lacked common ground, or was even painful. Among any of these variables, she may choose to not open to him again. It is important that she choose with self-awareness because she will be left with his impact.

Ellae: *"Your options for opening to a man range from sharing a casual 'Hello,' to a deep emotional, intellectual and spiritual sharing. Or merging with a man through orgasm. It is our right to choose."*

DISCONNECTING AND RECONNECTING

It is the nature of many men to be contained in their system of understanding. A religious man views the world through his theological beliefs, a scientist views the world through his scientific lens. Because of their sense of containment, men often feel the need to exit. This is especially true when a man has been inside of a woman's body. After this sharing, he is more balanced, and can return to his chosen system with increased productivity.

A man's exit has a great range. He may exit to take a short breather, go to work (his "system"). He might grow distant, move on, or just leave. Sometimes men become threatened by the intimacy of a relationship. It is important for a woman to pay attention to how a man exits, and his behavior thereafter. If he does not behave as a grateful guest and he is not a willing learner, then she has the choice to move on.

THE BEHAVIOR

Many women have fearful reactivity around when and how a man leaves and if he will come back. That fear of rejection rears its head all the time. It is so important for a woman to pay attention to how a man leaves and how he behaves after their intimate, emotional, or sexual encounter.

It is vital for a woman to step back, analyze, and determine how to reconnect with him in the future. Will she welcome him back? Or will she step back and ask for different behavior? Or step away? These decisions are hers alone to make. It is far more shaded than black and white. A woman can take as much time as she needs; there is no need to feel rushed by his drive or her own.

If the experience is painful or negative, she can choose to take time to go inside herself. Relish time in nature.

Look around.

See if there are any wise messages for you in the clouds, the flight of birds, the fresh clear air.

By finding a quiet place within, and using the techniques in this book, as well as those that she comes up with on her own, a woman can get clear, and decide how to move forward. It may be one step at a time or a clean break. If she needs to, she can choose to change. Self-knowledge is the goal.

When you know yourself then you know how to be in a great relationship.

A woman may also spend extra time in nature, take long bubble baths, do home facials, and give herself extra pampering and pleasure. Body grooming is a good retreat.

A woman does not need to spend a lot of time questioning and examining the man's exit behavior to understand him better. Instead, she can refocus her energy on her connection to Earth and building more in her own world. She can take the opportunity to discover how she is feeling, teach herself how to integrate this new self-knowledge, and relish in her own life.

Taking Your Energy Back

The next time your significant other leaves—whether to go get a coffee, in the midst of an argument, or even if he just left for good:

Take your energy off of him.
Bring it back to you.
Take a break.

Go for that outdoor breath.
Breathe.

Get the kids to bed.

Now...
What are you feeling?
What are your thoughts?
What are your current and immediate
needs in this moment?

It's all about you.

DENIED ENTRANCE

A woman often chooses to be with a man in order to increase her self-knowledge. A man chooses to be with a woman to enter connection through her body, access her instinctive wisdom, and experience her unique expression of femininity.

A man is in control of the exit while a woman is in charge of the entrance. Therefore women and men have discomfort and drama over the area they don't control. What happens when a woman has taken a man in deeply and she wants to release him, but he is not ready to go? When a man is denied entrance he feels inadequate and he often experiences fear, which manifests as emotional extremes.

It is important for a woman to focus on herself and her needs. She can start to seal off the entrances until he is on the periphery of her life. As she begins to deny the man entrance, a woman should be careful and respectful because this process can generate a lot of aggression. Relationships or marriages may experience painful chasms, divorce agony, or the other partner quickly finding a new mate. Even violence is a possibility.

How to Seal Off the Entrance

A woman can seal off her entrance by pushing the man more and more to the periphery of her life. She can do this by: no longer giving the man access to her body, getting a new job, getting another place to live, or getting a divorce attorney. If there are children, she will have to talk to them about the changes that are taking place. Each step will give her greater clarity about her decisions and next steps.

A woman in this situation may have many problems to solve and sacrifices to make. If she is certain in her desire to release him, she can take steps to push him to the periphery. This process may create challenges and provide opportunities for her to increase her self-knowledge and personal strength. The man may refuse to accept her choice and she should prepare to use all of the tools available to her in order to manage his refusal. Many abused women find themselves hiding from men who refuse to exit.

This is a complex and often frightening situation. One that requires professional help and guidance. Don't be afraid to ask for help and take it. Abusers isolate their victims. What they say and how they act are two different things. Break out of the habit of isolation and reach out. Talk to other women who have been there and have changed the circumstances of their life. Don't blame yourself. *Get help and get going.*

But once the man finally does accept it, the breakup develops a life of its own and the woman loses control of the separation. The man then typically leaves by his own choice.

LOVE IS ALWAYS AVAILABLE

A woman has an easy connection with Earth and understands this connection through her body. It is her pleasure to extend inspiration to the males in her life. This generosity helps her cultivate her optimistic femininity. You can absolutely make a guy's day by extending an unexpected smile. A radiant woman makes everyone feel better.

Instinctive wisdom is always guiding a woman towards reciprocity and Earth will always bring her into a state where love can roll through her and out to others. She is a source of renewal, constantly transforming what appears dead to new, burgeoning life and vitality. This is the gift of femininity.

CHAPTER TEN

THESE AMAZING BODIES

We live in these amazing bodies. Our bodies are consistent conveyors of receptivity, comfort, strength, inspiration, loveliness, and instinctive wisdom. The female body is the most desired, most competed for, and most beautiful vessel on Earth. Being so valuable creates great gifts as well as great problems.

The gifts include:
᳁ The very gift of being female, of giving life, of creating, of being desired, of having true, unchanging power.

Some of the problems include: The disgusting results of being ruled, restrained, abused, the curse of being raped, the horror of having free will taken away through being controlled, the embarrassment of having spontaneous instinctive wisdom debased or undervalued.

Perhaps the most undercutting problem is women competing with one another over the desirability of our bodies and physical beauty. We have a responsibility to use our body's power wisely. It doesn't help anyone to turn to petty competition or to use our bodies to make men feel insecure. We are greater than that.

We need to be in control of our bodies and our lives in order to protect this tremendous resource. Once we acknowledge Earth as our primary relationship, the calamities, difficulties, and negative competition surrounding our bodies that have previously afflicted us fall away. What remains is a devotion to live in reciprocity

A Woman's Sexual Power

The great sexual partners luxuriously explore us back to Earth.

Love Is All There Is

Our female body is love. When a woman orgasms, she is filled with love and that flows to her partner. She includes him in her ecstatic post-orgasm world no matter if she loves him in life or not. When we are fully in and with our body, love is all there is.

Sex For a Man

Many men find connection, fulfillment, relaxation, and relief through a woman's body. The rest of the time, they are in their contained, sometimes even isolated, rooms. For this reason, the drive to have sex can be consuming for a man.

The need to reconnect to the magnificent inner world of the woman and come out of the intense containment creates a man's great sexual sensitivity. Most men find the deepest amount of satisfaction when they reconnect and release through the body of a woman they love. For many men, this is true lovemaking.

Men who manipulate to get their sexual needs met have forgotten the gift of sex. Their hunger to connect can blind them from the reciprocal exchange. These men allow the experience to be all about them. It is a woman's responsibility to create a boundary and remind these men of the reciprocal gifts being exchanged.

It is all about love, respect, and reciprocity. This can end up being an idyllic experience, filled with pleasure, union, and fun. In great sex, both partners honor the gift of connection, excitation, release, and love given to them by Earth.

A Sharing

During sex, men and women share and give vital energies to one another. In this sharing, a balance occurs within the energy system of each partner, and the power of the orgasm can determine the depth of the sharing. In deep, generous sharing, both people are satisfied with the union.

After the time together, each can return to their individual lives, and both of them feel a difference. A man often feels renewed, balanced, and for a brief time, relaxed. In this state of temporary alignment, his ability to create systems that benefit the world increases.

Post-Coital Talk

After sex, a woman carries the energy of the man in her body. He has deposited his energy in his ejaculation and most women can feel it. For this reason, many women feel confusion or have difficulty with boundaries after intercourse. Because a woman tends to carry the man's energy inside of her, she often becomes the custodian of the energetic union and of the relationship. This means that she can feel the man's needs empathetically, often before she feels her own. She may strive to feel secure in her connection with this man because parts of his essence are still inside of her. If the relationship with the man is not this way for him, she may feel betrayed and angry. The anger is a way, sometimes desperate, to create the needed boundary.

This is why the woman wonders, "Will this go anywhere?" Then a woman's fear of rejection surfaces again. It is usually the woman who is filled with the potential of the relationship. It is the woman who most often feels she now carries a vulnerability to him that she didn't have before the sex. This can also be true for some men, but most commonly, men leave their energy in the woman and contain their personal boundaries unto themselves. Men go out into the world balanced, contained, and ready for the day. He leaves his partner retaining the union. Sex always has an emotional impact for a woman and often for a man this is just not the case.

DOES HE KNOW HOW TO NURTURE YOU?

It is useful for a woman to determine whether it is worth it to carry this man's energy inside of her. It is important for her to pose this simple question to herself, "Does he fulfill the qualities I am looking for in a man at this time?"

Reciprocity and reciprocal relating between men and women can become murky when it comes to sex. This is because during sex, the man typically gives the woman everything when he orgasms. The woman may do the same, but when the sex is over, the complete giving often goes through a metamorphosis because the needs of men and women vary.

Women carry the pleasure of connection alive within their bodies. Lovemaking fills us with happiness and connectedness. It feels like the right way to feel. After taking in the man, a woman typically expands the feelings from the lovemaking into some variation of a relationship. The natural response of a woman's body is to nurture their union and create more with him, not less. Unless the man and woman establish continuity, have a true commitment, or mutually agree on a respectful understanding of the relationship, the two may run into trouble.

Seldom does a woman have a sexual partner that she never thinks about again once the sex is over. From an unsatisfying casual sexual encounter to a satisfying union lasting for a lifetime, receiving the man sexually, particularly if both orgasm, will guarantee she retains his energy within her.

MANAGE THE IMPACT

The longer the sexual relationship, the more impacted the woman is likely to be by the man's energy. If this deep inner resonance with the man is not in her best interest, then it is time to clear her body. Some women practice abstinence, others wait for the connection to this man to wane and drain over time. The most effective response is to simply clear the body intentionally. If the encounter or encounters were highly emotional, clearing a man's energy from her body may take more time. No matter, clearing to get back to one's self is not only possible but personally enhancing. To not clear her body is to compromise herself!

"Don't compromise yourself…..you're all you've got."
JANIS JOPLIN

Through clearing her body and residing in it, she can more easily be herself; know her own mind and will. This valuable process of reclaiming herself provides the necessary distance to understand the impact the partner has left. She can choose whether she wants the connection again. She can govern the depth of any future union.

Ellae: "*If you think about it carefully why would anyone want to carry another's essence around? It furthers dependency. It is a full-time job to be a high-quality woman. To have the energy to meet the challenge of life, we must have a healthy containment first and then a strong ability to share meaning-fully as we choose. Wonderful long-term relationships develop autonomy and interdependence.*"

IT'S AN EMOTIONAL THING

For most women, the impact of sex is emotional, and so the woman's reactions are emotional. These emotions typically either create the ground for further closeness or a struggle to create distance.

Since the contact may not have been emotional for the man, when they discuss their relationship she feels like she speaks about togetherness, while he thinks and speaks in terms of measuring the space. In other words, he is either creating distance or proximity to her after the shared intimacy. Some men focus their energy on themselves and becoming autonomous: They move back into their lives. Other men become smothering and bombard the woman with attention. Neither of these behaviors embody true, reciprocal relating. If the woman wants a relationship with these men, she needs to teach them reciprocity. If he moves too far away, or comes too close, it is up to her to show him how to relate reciprocally.

If he takes distance, so does she. If he comes close, she can show him closeness without them absorbing one another. This confusion can take up an enormous amount of time and out of frustration, many women use men as entertainment, allowing their conversations among female friends to revolve around male relationships. While some of these conversations involve appreciation, others involve hashing over perceived inadequacies.

When women do this, they miss opportunities to discuss the process of personal integration. By using the experience as grist for the mill, like Earth, a woman can learn from a man's impact and choose to grow into greater autonomy.

Ellae: "*When a woman focuses too much energy on a man, she weakens her personal strength. She chooses to give herself and her power away. A woman can begin to feel as if she is walking around with only one high heel on.*"

If you find yourself giving large quantities of thoughts, emotions, and energy to a man in your present, your past, or your hopeful future, come back to the present. Celebrate and appreciate an element of nature in your immediate surroundings.

⟿ *Breathe into the lower half of your body.*

⟿ *Feel your longings inside you, and energize your body towards them.*

For example, if you enjoy your partner cooking for you, feel the strong sensations of this generosity and joy inside you. Your longings show you where you are going, and your body will manifest it and make it happen.

🎀 *Try:* Consciously choosing to integrate the man's impact, grow, and emerge with greater autonomy. Every time.

SEX AND THE POV OF THE MAN

A man may simply need sex and miss or fail to understand his partner's deep ability or desire for ongoing closeness. He may feel the woman's emotional demands and take space in order to reduce what feels like pressure for contact. He may seek time to integrate the experience in his own way. This can leave the woman feeling frustrated and she may feel that her personal needs are not being met.

Ellae: "For a single woman, it is entirely possible to experience a strange dichotomy. You know a partner is not long term. But the other side is you wonder about him, feel closer to him than is comfortable. This can be time consuming and not productive. Clearing your body allows the memories to be pleasant and the moving on easier.

"This vision of having a lovely, long-term relationship can be wonderful if the man shares the same vision, but painful if he doesn't. Whether or not the woman's desire to continue building a relationship is realistic or appropriate, when a man rejects her, she can feel unsupported, criticized, abandoned, unattractive, or forlorn. We understand. Each one of us has been there. Each disappointing experience adds up, creating layers of confusion and disappointment that can lead a woman to swear off intimacy and shut herself off from intimate love. Single or married."

For Autonomy to Exist

We are in our life for self-development. Self-development requires autonomy to exist and carrying another's energy prevents autonomy. First, clear the body. Second, contribute love to another type of relationship, perhaps with a family member or a pet. If we lose track of our autonomy we miss critical opportunities for essential self-development.

This is where the loss of innocence lies. This is where the loss of sweetness lies. It is here that our belief in the diminishing beauty of life and love begins. We are making our relationships the primary source for satisfying our desire to give and receive love, instead of Earth. We can't give if we are empty. Empathic connection will not bring us complete satisfaction. Remember your connection to Earth. Her energy flows will fill you up and renew you.

Reflect:

- ⊹ Do you keep Earth as your primary relationship?

- ⊹ Do you know how to put yourself first, gently but firmly? It is a good thing to learn.

- ⊹ Do you feel weighed down by disappointments in personal relationships?

If so, it's okay. We all struggle with it. Reinvent yourself. Set your intent. Move your intent into action. Start now.

CHAPTER ELEVEN
CLEAR OUR BODIES

TO CLEAR

Clearing after sex is only one time this skill is useful, even healthful.

A woman has the ability to use her body to feel the world and have empathy, compassion, and understanding for others. This power is true and wonderful, but the ability to have empathy can overwhelm us. A woman runs the risk of taking in too much information. Her husband's job challenges, her kid's scraped knee, her ex-boyfriend's illness, the wars of the world, the poverty. She can internalize emotions that were never intended for her.

The energies can fill her like a fog and she can feel clouded and murky. Thankfully, a woman can shift these sensations by clearing her body.

When a woman clears her body as regularly as she brushes her teeth, she can fully experience her own wonderful autonomy.

Many women have a natural urge to clear their bodies of excess energy and have developed various tactics in order to find clarity.

Some of these include:

- ↬ Exercising.
- ↬ Sleeping alone.
- ↬ Leading isolated lifestyles.
- ↬ Immersing in mental endeavors, but this means leaving the body and your strength.
- ↬ Choosing periods of celibacy.
- ↬ Having a good, long cry.
- ↬ Losing her temper.
- ↬ Body-based therapy.
- ↬ Lying on Earth each day; opening, breathing, and releasing all tension.
- ↬ Doing the yoga savasana, and when deeply relaxed, command her body to clear out all energies that are not hers.

When a woman has her own body, thoughts, and feelings she can experience true containment. It is useful to create this sense of safe containment without using anger as a tool. Many women use anger to create a boundary, but this can take a negative toll. Anger has its place, but it is like any power, it must be used carefully.

When a woman clears her body, she can thrive in marvelous reciprocal relationships. She claims her body as her own and can still experience empathy for loved ones. But her sensitivities become manageable and her autonomy strengthens. This book is full of suggestions for remembering your connection to Earth. These will assist you in clearing your body. The Rituals section also holds other ideas.

CHILDREN

When a woman gives birth, or chooses to adopt, she shares her body with her child. She can feel her children's needs and moods in her body. When the child is young and in danger, this is a valuable asset. But this can also place tremendous stress upon the woman.

When a woman excessively enmeshes herself in the lives of children and loved ones, she is out of balance with nature's laws. She loses her ability to know the boundaries of the mutual relationships between herself and others. She can begin to feel too much. Her life can become a sad dance, moving between being devoured and devouring.

THE CHOICE

A woman can choose when she wants to share her intense and valuable sensitivity. She can feel the emotional impact of her child and loved ones in her body and she can feel herself, her quality and her life. When she does choose to use her body to empathize with loved ones, she can still retain it for herself without getting depleted or sucked dry.

Through a deep remembering of her connection to Earth, she can respond reciprocally to everything that comes her way. She can live freely, feeling grounded and "self-contained" within her body and give to those she loves without becoming overwhelmed by needs and life's chaos.

WISDOM

In order to move forward in her autonomy and accomplish her life's destiny, a woman has to be an integrator. She needs to integrate each day, each experience into her body until the past exists only in mental memories, no longer in body feelings. These are the body feelings that we store in our bodies that no longer serve us. The painful breakup, the loss of a loved one, the speeding ticket from last month.

In gratitude, a woman can learn to release the past, and embrace the present moment. She can clear herself each day, using her own methods, or using some of the ideas we suggest in this book and realize her destiny. She can be an aquifer of reciprocity, which enables her to share her wisdom with the world. She can be the voice of Earth, a walking fountain of vitality.

CLEAR YOUR VESSEL

Your body is a vessel. You can easily clear it. Earth can help.

Sit on a patch of grass.

Greet Earth with a gift. Ask her to clear you.
Relax and let go.

Tend a flower bed.

Run your fingers through a river or slip your toes in the ocean.

Or just look outside your window. Gift. Admire. Be Grateful

Behold Nature's majesty.

Breathe Earth in. Let the stresses of the day
flow out on your exhale. Soften.

Focus on your immediate surroundings.

Notice . . . Birds Trees Sky

In this state of being deeply aware of . . .
Your body
Your emotions
Your thoughts
Relax. . .

Let go of your discomforts, your worries, and your task list.

Command your energy system to clear.

Ask Earth to clean you.

If it helps, you can envision water or sand draining down.

Drain the excess into Earth.
Let the unwanted energy leave.
You're cleansed. Renewed.

CHAPTER TWELVE
RITUALS

The ancients devised effective rituals that facilitate harmony both within oneself and within life. These rituals have been accumulated and honed through the centuries. Their genius lives in their ability to easily put humans in balance with the changes of Earth and the Universe. These were not done for the sake of tradition endeavoring to keep the past alive, but use nature's elements, verbal sound, music, rhythm, and personal intent. Through exquisitely orchestrated steps, the ritual brought individuals into alignment with Earth's resonance and energy flows. When alignment was achieved, a fluid harmony with life emerged.

In beauty happily I walk.
With beauty before me I walk.
With beauty behind me I walk.
With beauty below me I walk.
With beauty above me I walk.
With beauty all around me I walk.
It is finished again in beauty.
It is finished in beauty.

NAVAJO NIGHT CHANT

Many of these essential practices have been lost, replaced by the shell of rituals repeated for traditional purposes. These "replacement rituals" no longer convey the components needed to ensure harmony with life. Losing the original and deeper intent of the rituals has been a great disadvantage to humanity because these practices enable us to adapt gracefully to life changes while still remaining empowered, self-contained beings.

Ritual . . .

> Inspires reciprocal exchange.
> Offers an opportunity to incorporate the feast of life.
> Gives relief from the dull silence of conformity.
> Feeds Earth and nourishes her spirit.

When a woman does not use these rituals, she moves away from the ability to interpret every event as valuable. Her misalignment with the unfolding energies makes it easy for her to get into power struggles with life. It is often only in hindsight that she sees the value that was always there. When she aligns with Earth energies through ritual, she facilitates her discovery of the intrinsic value within every life event.

When she isn't in harmony with Earth's energy flows, it can take a long time to gain understanding of what is going on and to comprehend the situation's deeper causes and meanings. Over time, many opportunities for creative interaction get lost. What could be a valuable learning experience becomes a habitual response of excessive emotion or power struggle. The belief that "This should not have happened to me—life has made a mistake here" has become the normal human response to unwanted events. However, the longer we hold to that perception, the harder it is to move forward creatively.

RETURNING TO ESSENTIAL RITUALS

A woman can reinstate the art of ritual, using it as a tool to harmoniously facilitate change. Through ritual, a woman gains the strength of alignment with Earth, and when grounded, she is full of generosity and acceptance of all of the gifts that await her in her human endeavors.

To be effective, rituals have to be performed with a clear understanding of the correct elements. These elements need to be properly sequenced to bring about an alignment with the Earth. There is nothing more energetically touching than a properly performed ritual. It is humbling to arrange one's energies to blend with Earth's. It is inspiring to align one's intent with Earth's capacity for manifesting and this is the decisive value of ritual.

Rituals are not the dark use of energy, although there are rituals of darkness. Dark rituals are designed to guide or control an outcome, and a woman who performs them uses the Elements to get what she wants. But in these dark rituals, the spontaneous vibration of love is diminished because of the woman's exertion of control. The amount of love in any experience is related to how much control is being exercised. In control rituals, the outcome is an unavoidable cascading of negativity. Women who practice the controlling of energy, rather than intending to harmonize with it, fall prey to the diminishment of love.

Ritual Ideas

Rituals facilitate effective interaction with Earth's energies and seasonal changes. Here are a few Rituals that are easy to perform. They will help develop your personal interaction with Earth. These Rituals can be done for two minutes, two hours, or a whole day. They will put you in harmony with Earth. It is up to you and how you want to integrate them into your life.

Sleep Is a Ritual

The first and most essential ritual a woman must engage in is a good night's sleep. During sleep, humans are brought into reciprocity without effort. It is the only time that the body, mind, emotions, and spirit relax and align with the Universe. Not only is sleep a gift, but it is essential to support a life well lived. It is an act of spiritual commitment. Sleep is rebalancing. Balance is key. Humans sleep to restore ourselves from the rigors of life. Deep, uninterrupted sleep is vital. A woman cannot be true to her nature if she is either deprived of sleep or if she sleeps too long.

You can gauge the amount you personally require by experimenting. How much sleep do you need to be able to engage with life deeply, directly, and with the capacity for learning? Eight hours? Six? Nine? Proper sleep must be the first thing taken into consideration on the spiritual path or our capacity to learn dissipates. Life becomes one overwhelming experience after another.

A woman is confronted with millions of choices in her lifetime. Without a good, restful sleep, she has no chance of getting the break she needs to balance and gain the new perspective that can help her upgrade her life. When a woman is tired, she resides in the part of her nature that requires the least amount of effort; that aspect of herself that is the most predictable and familiar because she doesn't have the energy to do anything but the obvious. This puts her into a pattern of tedious repetition that drains her vitality and overshadows her dreams. She loses sight of her potential. She is reduced to a basic level of coping.

It is life itself that gives the learning she came here to do. When the learning starts, she needs to be ready. Sleep gets her to the starting gate.

Offerings to the Earth

Take yourself to a place in nature. Simply offer a gift of any kind to Earth: This is your way to honor and nurture her and is a wonderful way to develop a reciprocal relationship with her. One example is an offering of cornmeal or herbs. These are affordable, easily accessible, and they do not harm the Earth.

You can use anything you wish as an offering, as long as it won't do any environmental damage and is a gift that naturally decays. Earth eats the beauty of the sacrifice, the gift that you have given her.

Whatever the offering, the important thing is your sincere intention in giving the gift. Your intent to give thanks makes it a gift. Offer thanks as you give the offering and give gratitude to Earth for all that she provides.

The Eating Ritual

Prior to eating, when your food is in front of you, take a moment to place your hands around the food, or connect your energy to the food. Softly command that the food put itself in harmony with your body. You may wish to offer a prayer or some words of thanksgiving.

The Nurturing Ritual

Choose plants that you find beautiful and are comfortable with, and plant them inside or outside. It is important that the plant does not exceed your capacity to maintain it: You may not want to choose a high maintenance orchid, but instead choose a magnificent Creeping Charlie, which requires less attention and thrives on limited attention. Through nurturing a plant, you can come to understand the knowledge and wisdom that allow it to thrive. Pour yourself into its care and it will give back to you a hundredfold.

The Breathing Ritual

Take ten (or more) deep inhalations and exhalations. The importance lies in releasing and interacting with the breath. You may choose to focus on a certain area of the body that you feel needs nurturing, attention, or healing. You may want to visualize a favorite mountain, field, beach, or another place in nature to engage with its essence.

The Earth
Cleaning Ritual

Find a place outside and commit to walking in that area on a regular basis. Develop a personal relationship with all the qualities of Nature that encompass this place. Become very familiar with the area and the rhythms that are expressed there. Use your five senses and witness what the plants and the animals are doing, how they look, smell, feel, and interact. As you walk, expand your energy out. Ask Nature to clear you and she will.

After you have felt your field clear, draw your energy back to your body. A person's energy field obeys her commands and when you command your energy field to expand or enclose, it does.

Finish by firming up your energetic boundaries . . . "no one enters this space but me."

Beginnings and Endings

Beginnings: As you wake up in the morning, imagine yourself in the place you go to, to have Earth clear you. Allow yourself to remember your dreams from the night before. Ask Earth to clear you and open you to what the new day will bring.

Endings: Just before you go to bed, reflect on your day and where you put your time and energy. As you review each event, decide what you learned from it. Take in the learning and let the rest of the experience drift away on the wings of sleep. Welcome sleep. Invite your dream life to help direct your life. Ask that a question be answered by your dream and remember your dream in the morning. Your answer will be there.

FOCUSING ON THE DAY

As you get ready to launch into your day, ask what you intend to make come alive in life today. For example, you might want to dedicate your day to serving Earth by generating beauty in your own way. Your choice. You may want to incorporate the Breathing Ritual discussed earlier, or create your own. Give thanks to the generosity of Earth.

DISTRACTIONS

Develop a ritual committed to time away from your distractions. Go to your special place. Turn off the cell phone. Calm your mind by focusing on your five senses. Choose one sense and expand it out into your place. Feel your stress drain out; sand returning to the Earth. Your sense of presence returns.

CHI GONG EXERCISES

Chi Gong done daily is an example of a Ritual whose form provides a free inner space to unite with the ever-changing energy.

Chi Gong provides a solid outer structure that enables placement for an ever-changing inner energetic reality to exist. The Chi Gong Exercises, discussed in Chapter Four, can also be practiced as Ritual.

Nurture Earth Ritual

I will use the example of an oil tanker spill on Earth. When oil spills and damages Earth and her creatures, it is like having a dear, dear friend in the hospital. Your friend is hemorrhaging and the blood loss has not been stoppable. Throughout the body, the suffocating flow is responsible for vital cells being killed.

Your friend needs to be comforted and encouraged while navigating through this crisis to return to balance and strength. You are not a medical or scientific professional, but you are a wonderful friend committed to healing and well being. How would you respond to your friend's struggle?

This is the question I have been posing for myself. Unable to live in complete daily detachment, I longed to find a way to be a part of Earth's challenge and a part of the solution. This has been my way, and perhaps it will help you find yours.

Learn to be very aware of your contact with the Earth under your feet, as you lean against a tree, or share amazement at the beauty of a bug. Know that you are simultaneously encouraging, admiring, and comforting Earth.

We all know the 50 things we can do to help Earth practically. Essential things. Now we know 51.

Winter Solstice

The ultimate ritual is Winter Solstice. An effective Solstice ceremony moves us away from the world's demands and harmonizes us with Earth. The ritual should generate momentum among its attendants and inspire them to integrate the old, empty the past, and completely open to the new.

The ritual is to be performed on the right day and dovetail with the precise time of Solstice, when Earth's energies change to be concordant with the new year ahead. Solstice creates harmonic convergence with the upcoming changes that the new year will bring. For the ancients, Solstice was considered the time to completely finish the past by integrating each bygone event to glean its gift of wisdom. And then plant the seeds of the new year and signify a new life. When the Winter Solstice is celebrated, Earth, aligning herself at that time, is happy to facilitate you. She will take you along, flowing you from what has been to what you are and will be creating. On this most powerful day, an effective ritual will bring you into energetic harmony.

REALIGN WITH EARTH'S RESONANCE

Use this Ritual on the Winter Solstice and practice it any time of the year. Putting yourself into the flow of the Earth's harmony on this day can be an important exercise that will assist you throughout the next twelve months.

Remove yourself completely from the noises and demands of the world. Sit quietly and allow your physical senses to flow outward, until you feel calm and empty. Now think of Earth by thinking of Nature. Feel your attachment to Nature, from her vegetation and animals, to the flow of her waters and the strength of her rocks. Release your demands on everyone who came into your life this year so they are free to move in whatever direction they choose. Then, one by one, reintroduce your senses.

- ↬ Touch
- ↬ Smell
- ↬ Taste
- ↬ Hearing
- ↬ Seeing
- ↬ Reintroduce your hearing.
- ↬ Slowly open your eyes.
- ↬ Light a single candle and let its radiance bathe across your face.

Remind yourself that you are an important member of the Universal Family. Realize that your position here is exactly what it is supposed to be. Your role is important and you are needed in the fabric of the Universal Whole. Feel yourself fall into peaceful harmony with all of life.[1]

---

1. This ritual is adapted from the work of Gregge Tiffen. See http://www.g-systems.com/cgi-bin/essays.cgi?submit=ViewEntry&month=Decembe r&year=2007&file=30-14.35.53.txt

CHAPTER THIRTEEN

EARTH AND YOU

Today there is scientific evidence that the Earth is changing. Our Earth is changing and she has a phenomenal capacity to regenerate herself. We can help her in this process of regeneration and renewal. And continue to encourage her to generate life that supports quality life for all.

Through connecting with the Earth's resonance and developing our own deep, nurturing relationship with her, we can help in her natural rebalancing. When women nurture a close relationship with Earth, we sense her nature. We then speak naturally for her. We know instinctively what Earth needs. We speak up, and we are heard.

We have provided many examples of honing and deepening our relationship with Earth and her resonance such as Chi Gong, meditation, walks in nature, dance, and practicing rituals. But the best way for you to cultivate this relationship is to discover your own unique way to connect into her and her vibrations, and to appreciate her beauty. She feeds you with her beauty and you feed her with yours.

Earth will then tell you what she needs and how you can use your own (exceptional) unique talents and gifts to help her heal. She engages us continually and needs us to speak for her. So ask yourself:

- ✧ What do you intend to do to make Earth come alive today?
- ✧ How do you intend to generate beauty today?
- ✧ Contemplate the power behind the beauty.

This is you.

You are her voice.

ABOUT THE AUTHORS

Ellae Elinwood

A well-known teacher of optimum health and well-being, Ellae draws upon a background rich in varied experience. For many years she was an instructor of Hatha Yoga, privately, and at colleges, universities, and fitness spas throughout Southern California. She pioneered a program teaching yoga to the elderly in convalescent homes, *Forever Young, A New Health Approach to Our Aged*, that was televised nationally.

Through her studies of yoga, ancient wisdom, and investigation into the effects of energy systems and emotions on the face, Ellae developed her comprehensive facial toning exercise program that was published in her book *Timeless Face* (St. Martin's Press, 1999). In this book, she demonstrates how many of the facial features of aging are actually symptoms of emotional distress and lack of facial fitness, which can be corrected through the book's program of toning, acupressure, and self-awareness.

She has inherited from her Celtic ancestors a gift of great intuition. As a result, she has shared her gift with thousands of clients over the last 25 years.

As an outgrowth of her background and her commitment to the Earth, she gives seminars on the topics expressed in this book. Ellae has recently launched a new educational program: H.E.R. (Helping Earth Rebalance). More information on H.E.R.'s dynamic, classes, seminars, and personal sessions can be found at HelpingEarthRebalance.com.

Books by Ellae Elinwood:

Timeless Face (1999), *The Everything T'ai Chi and Qigong Book* (2002), *Stay Young With T'ai Chi* (2003), *The Everything Numerology Book* (2003), *Qigong Basics* (2004)

Dr. Mary Lanier

Dr. Mary Lanier is a proud mother of three who holds a Master of Arts in Psychology and a Ph.D in Spiritual Studies. Mary worked for twenty-five years as a psychotherapist in Missouri, California, and Paris, France, while concurrently being a consultant and trainer for several corporations and international organizations.

In her forties, a health crisis helped her rediscover her connection to the planet by studying meditation and spending time in nature. She healed her ailments and aligned with her purpose: to be a voice of Earth.

Going Mobile with
Earth is Your Sweet Spot

Want to keep the message of *Earth is Your Sweet Spot* in your life? Then get it in the Q*—a simple way of bringing what you want into your life.

A Remembrance

Ellae Elinwood reminds us of our connection with Earth in her own voice and offers it in a FREE deck of Q*z for your computer or smart phone. Carry it with you as a mobile meditation.

www.qcardz.com/earthisyoursweetspot

Daily Activation

Activate your connection to Earth in a moment with these peaceful mobile reminders. Register at www.qcardz.com and access a FREE deck of EYSS 'Daily Activation' Q*z ($4.99 value).

Getting it in the Q*

Register at www.qcardz.

Then choose your Q*z.

To get Q*z on your iPhone, download the FREE Q*Cardz app at the iTunes App Store.

For more information about Q*z, visit www.qcardz.com